P(OF)OWER TWELVE

GARY WATTERS

WESTBOW
PRESS®
A DIVISION OF THOMAS NELSON
& ZONDERVAN

This book is a work of non-fiction. Unless otherwise noted, the author and the publisher make no explicit guarantees as to the accuracy of the information contained in this book and in some cases, names of people and places have been altered to protect their privacy.

WestBow Press books may be ordered through booksellers or by contacting:

WestBow Press
A Division of Thomas Nelson & Zondervan
1663 Liberty Drive
Bloomington, IN 47403
www.westbowpress.com
844-714-3454

Scripture quotations marked KJV are taken from the King James Version.

Scripture quotations marked NIV are taken from The Holy Bible, New International Version®, NIV® Copyright © 1973, 1978, 1984, 2011 by Biblica, Inc.® Used by permission. All rights reserved worldwide.

ISBN: 978-1-6642-1142-1 (sc)
ISBN: 978-1-6642-1143-8 (hc)
ISBN: 978-1-6642-1141-4 (e)

Library of Congress Control Number: 2020921663

Print information available on the last page.

WestBow Press rev. date: 11/19/2020

PREFACE

She was eighty-three years old. Her body had been ravished by disease for almost sixty years. Every day was marked by pain, yet every day Corene Watters began with Psalm 118:24: "This is the day the Lord has made, rejoice and be glad in it." Why did she begin her day this way? She felt that a proper attitude of gratitude—a thankful approach to the positives in life—was certainly better than dealing with the negatives.

That philosophy was passed on to a thankful son who understood that the wisdom found in this verse was only one of many examples of wisdom found in the Bible. In fact, it led me to believe that the secret to a happy and successful life is contained in this book. It is not only a Christian's guide to happiness and success, but it is also a guide for all to follow. Whether you seek strength, love, peace, wisdom, endurance, humility, hope, faith, guidance, purpose, abundance, confidence, or gratitude, you can find it in scriptures.

It was the guide to Father Abraham thousands of years ago. It was the guide to Moses and David in the Old Testament and to the apostles of the New Testament. It has continued to guide men and women of past generations and will guide future generations.

This book reflects many valuable principles, as the book is littered with Bible verses throughout each chapter. It is my hope that as you read these pearls of wisdom, you will be able to apply a few of them to your life. In so doing, you will make your life and the lives of those around you a little happier and a little more successful.

CONTENTS

STRENGTH

But they that wait apon the Lord shall renew their strength;
they shall mount up with wings as eagles; they shall run,
and not be weary, and they shall walk and not faint.

—Isaiah 40:31

The easy answer for how to renew your strength and your energy is found in the first phrase of the verse: "wait upon the Lord." Our faith and trust in God will renew us daily.

Look at Isaiah. For the first thirty-nine chapters, he preached repentance without success. Through the reigns of four kings (Uzziah, Jotham, Ahaz, and Hezekiah) and spanning forty years (740–700 BC), Isaiah spoke out against apostasy, idolatry, immorality, and political and social corruption. The nation of Judah failed to turn back to God. Isaiah himself prophesied that indeed the nation would not heed his words, and this would lead to judgment and banishment for the nation.

"Then said I, Lord, how long? And he answered, until the cities be wasted without inhabitant, and the houses without man, and the land be utterly desolate. And the Lord have removed men far away, and there be a great forsaking in the midst of the land."[1] His prophecies would foretell the utter destruction of a nation and most of its inhabitants. The brutality of Assyrian invasions and failure of Isaiah's preaching would cause most people to quit and give up. Yet here in chapter 40 we see one of the most inspirational verses in the Bible. Following the first thirty-nine chapters that deal with judgment, we begin to see prophecies that radiate with hope of renewal, restoration, and salvation.

---

[1] Isaiah 6:11–12.

How do we mount up with wings like eagles? We can always mount up with wings like eagles by waiting on the Lord, by trusting in the Lord, by seeking his guidance, and by following his lead. "The Lord is my strength and my shield; my heart trusted in him and I am helped; Therefore my heart greatly rejoiceth, and with my song I will praise him."[2] Praising God for renewed strength is something that should be done daily. As I dig into this verse, I see the full life of a Christian revealed. I see the excitement and possibilities of youth in the line "they shall mount up with wings like eagles." I see the wisdom and purpose of middle age in the line "they shall run and not be weary." And I see the satisfaction of completing the race in the line "they shall walk and not faint."

The story of David and Goliath is one of the great stories of the Bible. On one mountaintop you have the mighty Philistines, and on the other mountaintop you have the army of Israel. The Philistines sent out their champion, Goliath of Gath, a mighty man who stood over nine feet tall. His armor alone weighed 125 pounds. His spear was like a weaver's beam, and the head of the spear weighed fifteen pounds. The challenge went out to come and fight. Israel's reaction and that of their leader, Saul, was expected; they were afraid.

Enter David—the youngest of eight sons of Jesse. David was too young for battle. He stayed at home to feed his father's sheep. For forty days the Philistines called out and challenged the Israelites, and for forty days the Israelites refused to fight. Finally, Jesse, by the way of David, sent food to David's older brothers. David heard the challenge and asked a question: "Who is this uncircumcised Philistine that he should defy the armies of the living God?"[3] A young David saw that with God all things are possible, and David approached Saul and said that he would fight Goliath.

Saul looked at things through the eyes of a general: David was but a youth, and the Philistine a man of war and a giant at that. Yet David was persuasive. He told of his exploits, how he had protected the sheep and slain both a lion and a bear, and that the living God would deliver him against the Philistine. The young David took a slingshot and five smooth stones and went out without armor to face the Philistine.

The Philistine looked at David with disgust and disdain. What kind of battle would this be? The Philistine cursed David and pledged to feed his flesh to the fowls of the air and the beasts of the field. At this point

David rose up with the wings of eagles and gave us one of the great battle cries of history: "Thou comest to me with a sword and with a spear and with a shield; But I come to thee in the name of the Lord of Hosts, The God of the armies of Israel, whom thou has defied. This day will the Lord deliver thee into mine hand. For the battle is the Lord's and he will give you into our hands."[5]

We all know the rest of the story. One small stone properly placed on Goliath's forehead and the battle was won, and the Philistines fled. There would be many more exploits in the life of David, but it was his trust and faith in God that allowed David to rise up with wings like eagles. He believed God was with him. Everyone feared Goliath but not David because he knew that God's powers could conquer any fear. Do you have a Goliath in your life? Let God's power give you the courage to win the victory and rise up on eagle's wings.

It is not surprising that the book of Psalms talks about the Lord's strength over eighty times. The songs of David bear repeating. Where do you get your strength? Look to David and look to the Psalms.

I will love thee, O Lord my strength.[6]

God is our refuge and strength, a very present help in trouble.[7]

Unto thee, O my strength, will I sing, for God is my defense, and the God of my mercy.[8]

Bow down thine ear to me; deliver me speedily; be thou my strong rock, and a house of deference to save me.[9]

David knew where his strength came from. When I was seventeen, I witnessed a young man like David tackle his Goliath. Charles was twenty years old, small in stature, insecure around people, and had the most severe stuttering problem I have ever heard. It was impossible to carry on a conversation with him, and as an arrogant seventeen-year-old, I simply shied away from him. I dismissed his value, his speech, his social skills, his and physical appearance, and I even questioned his mental capacity. What I did not understand was his love of the Lord and how God can turn weakness into strengths. "My grace is sufficient for you; my power is made perfect in weakness."[10] Charles was not impressive, but he would become influential.

One Sunday morning Charles walked the aisles of the church and announced that with the Lord's help, he wanted to be a preacher. My first thought was that Charles had lost it, and he would only further embarrass himself and his family. Charles was being set up to fail. But faith never fails a person; we fail when we give up on our faith. We tend to think God wants to only use the best—our strengths—but he also wants to use our weaknesses. Remember that God is never limited by our limitations. "The excellency of the power may be of God and not of us."[11]

I could not wait for that Sunday when Charles was scheduled to stutter through the sermon. A complete row of teenagers eagerly anticipated the "show." That day God's power and glory was made manifest in the life of Charles. He rose up with wings as eagles and delivered a great message. Not once did he stutter. Charles would go on to become a particularly good evangelist. His stuttering affliction was still there as part of a normal conversation, but when he talked about God, his speech was clear and concise.

"They shall run and not be weary." Just two verses before Isaiah 40:31, we read another inspirational passage: "He giveth power to the faint and to them that have no might He increaseth strength."[12] When Paul was blinded on the Damascus road, he was left weak and totally dependent on others. He went from the proud and persecuting Saul to the humble, helpless Paul. He went from the persecutor of Christians to become the man God chose to evangelize the Roman world.

Perhaps it was the persecution and inquisition of the early church that made him so zealous. He immediately began his life mission, and as you view his missionary journeys you understand that through the strength of God, he ran and did not grow weary. That first missionary journey included Cypress, Perga, Antioch, Iconium, Lystra, and Derbe. A second and third missionary journey took him all over the Roman world. Obviously, his impact cannot be understated.

Let us lay aside every weight, and the sin that doth so easily be set us, and let us run with patience the race that is set before us.[13]

Let us not be weary in well doing, for in due season we shall reap if we faint not.[14]

Paul ran the race; he did not grow weary. Even in a martyred death, Paul found strength in the Lord. Paul's burning zeal, untiring industry, singleness of purpose, patient suffering, and sublime courage can be traced to the power of his faith. "For God is the strength of my heart, and portion forever."[15]

Moses was eighty years old when God called him out of the desert to lead the Jewish people from Egyptian bondage. The classic movie *The Ten Commandments* tells the story of Moses and his people so well. What I remember most about that picture was Moses walking and, by the power of God, not fainting. He walked through the desert, he walked back to Egypt, he walked and led the people through the Red Sea, he walked up mountains to receive the Ten Commandments, and he walked back down again. Through all his struggles he did not faint. He stayed on task for God.

It was eighty years before God used Moses. You should prepare yourself to live to be one hundred and be prepared to be strengthened by God, for he will renew your strength. He will help you to walk and not grow faint, and he may want your service when you can no longer fly like an eagle or run like a deer, but recalling the story of the tortoise and the hare, you can still win the race.

What happens when the adversities of life seem to take your strength, and you question the strength of the Lord? Remember that you can choose what your problem will do to you. No one is exempt from the challenges of life. Every mountain has its peak and every valley has its low point. We are all going to face ups and downs in this life, but we do not have to face them alone.

The Lord will always be there no matter what your circumstances. The Lord can help you level out the mountain peaks and can walk through the lowest valleys with you. When all things seem lost, your mountains can be conquered through faith. Jesus provides us lessons in saving faith.

> If you have faith as a grain of a mustard seed, you shall say unto this mountain, remove hence to yonder place and it shall remove; and nothing shall be impossible unto you.[16]

> Every mountain and hill shall be made low.[17]

I have recently received great inspiration from the story of Jim Kelly. Kelly led the Buffalo Bills to four Super Bowls, and his leadership on and off the field has been admired by many. Yet it is his recent struggle with cancer that has touched the lives of so many. This affliction has brought him near death, yet his faith provides us another example of the power of God. "O Lord, my strength and my fortress, and my refuge in the day of affliction."[18]

Mr. Kelly started a program called Kelly Tough and attributes his rise from near death to life to the strength he received through prayers and an attitude of "I will not quit. I will walk and not grow faint." Jim Kelly is Kelly Tough because he has found strength in his faith, through the power of prayer and the support of others. One of the more popular songs in Christian music today is "Everlasting God," by Chris Tomlin. The first lyric, "Strength will rise as we wait upon the Lord," epitomizes what Jim Kelly has found to be true. It has brought glory to the Lord and become an inspiration and a hope for many.

We are not promised that our skies will be sunny, but God promises to see us through. Every battle we face can be won when we turn our lives over to God. "For if God is for us, who can be against us."[19] Even in death, we can have the victory for we are promised eternal life for all who believe in Jesus Christ. For the people who have lived their lives where God has been their fortress, their refuge, and their strength, this promise provides us a special look at the light behind the shadow.

The journey of life does not always take a straight road. There are many twists and turns. Sometimes it's an interstate highway, and sometimes it becomes a muddy trail. When we are not focused, when we attempt to navigate the road alone, and when we think our strength is enough to see us through, we can become frustrated, anxious, worried, fearful, depressed, and stressed. These are all negative emotions that can bring you down and get you stuck in the mudhole of life.

God offers a better alternative. He offers his strength and his power to overcome. When my days are finished, I want to know that I finished the race strong. I want to identify with the inspirational verse written by Isaiah twenty-seven hundred years ago. "They that wait upon the Lord shall renew their strength; they shall mount up with wings as eagles; they shall run and not be weary, and they shall walk and not faint."[20]

LOVE

A new commandment I give unto you, that you love one another, as
I have loved you, that ye also love one another. By this shall all men
know that you are my disciplines, if ye have love one to another. 1
—John 13:34–35

God is love. This powerful truth changed the world, keeps on changing the world, and can change your own world. God's love is seen in his character, his saving activity in his character, his saving activity in the world, and his people. The gospels, particularly the writings of John, remind us that God is the source of love. Furthermore, the love of God is not an abstract love. It is a visible manifestation of God's character seen in the life, death, burial, and resurrection of Jesus Christ. Those who know God realize that God's love is transformational, and the love that we show others is a validation of our faith.

The phrase *I love you* is said to contain the three most powerful words in the English language, and yet the word *love* is one of the more casually used words in our language. I love basketball, I love a ribeye steak, I love to ski, and on it goes. But the love of God is different. His is an agape love, a sacrificial love that one can only experience and understand through a relationship in Jesus Christ. To better understand the command to love one another and recognize how understanding that command can change one's life, one must first understand God's love for us. "While we were yet sinners Christ died for us."[2] Sin separates us from a righteous God, yet he loves us, though we do not deserve that love. He showers us with his grace, and that love was expressed when he sent his only Son that we might know him and feel the depth of his love.

By loving one another, we show our love for God and show that God lives within us, because the love we extend to others is grounded in God's love. The invisible God lives and loves through us. Through the indwelling of the Holy Spirit we are able to love others, because the "fruit of the spirit is love."[3] As we mature, our love is perfected and our growth in God's love gives us confidence about our status as God's children. Those who have lived in the love of God need have no fear, as there is "no fear in love; but perfect love casteth out fear."[4]

Think about the blessing you receive by loving others. We have the love of God shown through Jesus. We have the Holy Spirit within us that gives us the capability to love others as God loves. We also have no fear because of God's love. Remember that every love we express toward God and toward other people comes only in response to our prior experience of his love. When we are empowered by God's love, we believers will reflect God's character by showing love to one another.

So where do you stand on loving others, and how do you put that love into action by helping others? John Wooden, the great basketball coach of UCLA, was not only an iconic coach but a wonderful teacher of life lessons. A specific guide to his success was the principle of helping others. "You have not lived a perfect day until you have done something for somebody who cannot repay you." Have you lived a perfect day? When you help other people, you help yourself as well. We were placed on this earth for two purposes: to love and serve God, and to love and help one another. Over fifty references in the New Testament alone are about these two commandments. "Thou shalt love the Lord thy God with all thy heart, all your soul, and with all your mind. This is the first and great commandment and the second is like unto it, thou shalt love thy neighbor as thyself."[5] When we follow these commands, we not only honor God and help others, we help ourselves.

Let me give you a personal example. Twenty years ago, on a Saturday night before Christmas, I officiated a basketball game some forty-five miles from my home. I left the gym about 10:00 p.m., got in my car, and started the long drive home alone, and believe me it is one of the longest forty-five minute drives one can take with no towns in between and few lights—just miles and miles of prairie. As I was leaving town, I saw a hitchhiker. I don't normally stop for hitchhikers, but something on that cold December night said stop. The man that got in my car had just gotten out of the county jail, a place he had called home for six months. That was a little unsettling to me, but he seemed very thankful that someone had picked him up after he had spent four hours in the winter cold. Our trip across the dark landscape of northern Oklahoma began with some anxiety on my part, but a silent prayer seemed to ease that anxiety, and our conversation turned to Christmas and its true meaning.

As we rode along I learned that he lived in my hometown and that he had a wife and a new baby that he had not yet seen. We talked about why I had picked up a stranger and about the love we are to have for others. "The stranger that dwelleth with you shall be unto you as one born among you, and thou shalt love him as thyself."[6] As he got out of the car at a small little duplex in a poorer part of town, we saw a Christmas tree in the window. His parting words were, "I will never forget your kindness, and this will be a special Christmas." That was a perfect day, but who received the greatest blessing? I would argue that it was me. Twenty years later, I still receive blessings from that act of kindness. I believe success in life is often measured by what we do for others.

Danny Thomas, the wonderful comedian of early television, had a vision—a vision to help people to help unfortunate children suffering from various diseases. Thomas understood that real success was found in helping others, and countless lives have benefited from that vision. St. Jude Children's Hospital is a result of Mr. Thomas's vision and his willingness to understand this biblical principle and command: "This commandment we have from Him, that he who loveth God love his brother also."[7]

I have coached youth sports for almost forty years and have discovered team sports to be a great conveyor of this life principle. A coach can teach the fundamentals of the game. A coach can help the players understand the game. A coach can provide the physical training to put a player in shape to play the game. However, the most important job a coach has is to inspire to lift everyone on the team so that you can make everyone's dreams come true.

Greed and selfishness can ruin a team. All the great teams successfully answer one question: "What can I do to help my teammates achieve their goal?" That type of attitude causes a team to be successful and bring honor to all. Larry Bird is considered one of the greatest basketball players of all time. His individual skills have been matched by only a handful of players, but what set him apart was his ability to make everyone around him better. The genuinely great teams are teams guided by the biblical command, "by love serve one another."[8] We are born to influence and serve. I was impressed the other day when I heard current NBA star Kevin Durant say, "I want to be a better teammate and help my brothers achieve success." People of true greatness are always lifting others up.

Is there something to the biblical truth to love one another? You bet! Is there something to having a willingness to serve? Look at the life of Christ—the suffering servant—and his message in the Sermon on the Mount: "Whosoever shall compel thee to go a mile, go with him twain."[9] Decide today to accommodate people who ask you for a favor. Be willing to go the extra mile. Going the extra mile may be the key to your success. For by giving, sharing, and going the extra mile, you have created opportunities for others to grow and live. "Look not every man on his own things, but every man also on the things of others."[10]

The classic movie *Ben Hur* has a wonderful scene that explains the benefit of helping others. An old man who no longer can walk is paired with a younger, stronger man who no longer can see. Together they make a great team, as one becomes the other's legs, and the old man becomes the young man's eyes. You know, great things can happen through a person who doesn't care who gets the credit. Would you rather succeed and share the glory or fail and bear the blame alone? We are all weak in some areas, but when we allow others into our lives, we benefit and grow, so that our weaknesses become strengths.

Can we love one another without respecting one another? We know the biblical principle to love and help others, but do we respect others? "Honor all men, love the brotherhood."[11] I believe we are to respect the people with whom we live, work, and relate to. God loved us and thought enough about us to send his Son, and the Lord entreats us to love one another as he has loved us. Something beautiful is in every person.

I am reminded of the story of the good Samaritan. The rabbi and the priest walked past, but the stranger showed mercy. He picked the man up, bandaged his wounds, and left him in good hands. He went the extra mile. He showed the mercy we are to show. He respected a person not of his race. Our world today is filled with so many people hurting, and we have no excuses for not touching with healing love. "For I was an hungered and ye gave me meat, thirsty and ye gave me a drink, I was a stranger and ye took me in … In as much as you did it to one of the least of these my brethren, ye have done it unto me."[12] When we focus on human needs rather than selfish pleasure we become more fulfilled and satisfied as an individual, because we fill someone else's cup. Self-serving and self-seeking is ultimately self-defeating. If you want satisfaction and spiritual prosperity, commit yourself in service to others. Remember Isaiah's cry, "Here am I, send me."[13] I believe that everyday God wants to speak to someone through your life.

It is so easy to be selfish. It is one of my greatest sins. I blame it on being an only child—of having a mother who made me feel I was the only thing important in this world. Lord help me overcome selfishness; Lord help me become humble. "Let nothing be done through strife or vain glory; but in lowliness of mind let each esteem others better than themselves."[14] Looking out after your personal interests is proper life management, but when we do so at the exclusion of others it is selfishness. Love is not selfish; love builds up relationships. "For even the son of man came not to be ministered unto, but to minister."[15]

Cultivating relationships is so important. We need each other; we are designed for companionship. "And if one prevail against him, two shall withstand him, and a threefold cord is not quickly broken."[16] Your relationships will change as God's love in you overflows to others. You will become a channel of God's love and discover your role in life. Remember, life is meant to be shared.

A relationship rooted in the love of God is designed to succeed. It is a relationship in which we love one another, we encourage each other, we serve each other, we teach each other, we accept each other, and we pray for each other. This is a relationship not only designed for this life but for eternal life. Jesus Christ provided the best example as you examine his relationship with his disciples. He was always concerned with their welfare. Jesus instructed them and ultimately laid down his life for them. They in turn were willing to lay down their lives for him. Ten of the twelve disciples were eventually martyred. "As I have loved you, ye also love one another."[17]

Jesus made friends an art. You do so by cultivating close, meaningful relationships. Friends help each other; they don't use each other. Friends encourage each other; they don't discourage each other. In describing a good friend, Albert Camus said, "Don't walk in front of me I may not follow, don't walk behind me, I may not lead. Just walk beside me and be my friend." Oprah Winfrey, once said, "Lots of people want to ride with you in the limo, but what you want is someone who will take the bus with you when the limo breaks down."

As we examine the scripture and the command to love one another as Christ has loved us, it is that sacrificial love that we come to understand and appreciate through the influence of the Holy Spirit, and we must realize its importance to a Christian. Love is the highest characteristic of God; it is one attribute in which all other characteristics harmoniously blend. The gracious love of God to humankind underlies all that he has done and is doing. Love is the preeminent virtue of Christianity.

"By this shall all men know that ye are my disciples, that ye have love one to another."[18] This is what separates Christianity from other faiths—the sacrificial love of Christ—and we as Christians are identified by the love that others can see in us. Our purpose in life is to love God, honor God, love others, and serve others. In this way, you will know us, that we love one another. Two scriptures in Deuteronomy seem to be a proper way to close this chapter.

> Thou shalt love the Lord thy God with all thine heart, with all thy soul, and with all thy might.[19]

> And he will love thee, bless thee, and multiply thee.[20]

This promise from God sustains me and will guide me into a promising future.

PEACE

Be careful for nothing; but in everything by prayer and supplication
with thanksgiving, let your request be made known and unto
God. And the peace of God which passeth all understanding
shall keep your hearts and minds through Christ Jesus.
—Philippians 4:6–7

In the song, "The Beat Goes On," by Sonny and Cher, there is the lyric "men still keep marching off to war," yet the beat goes on. The band U2, in their classic hit "Sunday Bloody Sunday," echoes out the chant: "And the battles just begun, there are many lost but tell me who has won," yet the beat goes on. Edwin Starr in the anthem "War" asks and answers the question about war: "What is it good for, absolutely nothing," yet war drums continue to beat across this old world. Even the prophet Jeremiah cried out, "Peace, peace, when there is no peace."[1]

In the seventh grade, and in the middle of a nuclear arms race between Russia and the United States, I can remember practicing hiding under a desk in case of a nuclear holocaust. We have witnessed wars or the threat of wars throughout our lifetime, no matter what your age. The treaty between England and Germany before World War II was to achieve "peace in our time," and yet seven years later the world had over fifty million deaths attributed to World War II. Four years later, the Korean War would scar our world with more deaths and leave us with a peninsula that remains in turmoil sixty-five years later. We have experienced a cold war that saw proliferation of nuclear weapons and incidents that brought us to the Vietnam War. This was a war that internally ripped our nation apart and took the lives of some fifty-eight thousand American soldiers in a far-off land in Southeast Asia. In recent years we have seen our young men fight in Afghanistan and Iraq. We have watched civil war essentially destroy the country of Syria and seen Israel and Iran rattle their military swords and threaten one another with disaster, yet the beat goes on.

We all know that in war there are no winners, and in peace there are no losers, yet mankind seems to continually have a difficult time achieving peace. The question is why, and what can we do about it? One can point to the lack of fairness, the lack of justice, or the inequality that exists in the world. While many in the United States sit comfortably in their homes surrounded by all the "things" that seem to make life better, suffering occurs in every corner of this world and in our own country. The immigration crisis that has seen many people from Honduras and Guatemala show up on our southern border and the immigrants from Syria and other Middle East countries that have shown up in countries throughout Europe speak to injustice, to inequality, and to the ultimate unfairness that exists in this world.

Religious rivalries over beliefs and teachings have interrupted our pursuit of the one true God. When a suicide bomber kills over fifty innocents in the name of Allah, something is seriously wrong. Ethnic differences cause mistrust and jealousies that lead to further turmoil. The creation of class barriers, economic inequalities and societies that seek to protect the few rather than the many all have led to turmoil and our inability to achieve everlasting peace.

These are all man-made problems. Our real problem is that we have left God on the sidelines. We have created our own path, and it is not the path we were intended to travel. The result has been conflict—war and rumors of war. The solution is found in the Bible. All of God's conditions for peace are laid out in the Bible. There are plans that lead to peace, but when we reject God's peace, we reject peace altogether. Without God, our leaders can never find permanent peace. "The way of peace they do not know, there is no judgment in their goings. They have made them crooked paths; whosoever goeth therein shall not know peace."[2]

How do we as a people receive this wonderful gift—this gift of peace? First, understand that peace is a state of tranquility, a quietness of spirit that transcends any circumstance. It is a gift, one of the gifts the Holy Spirit brings to us, one that not only benefits us but is there to share with others. The closer we draw to God, the more peace we enjoy. When we develop a lifestyle of making God our refuge, we come to draw near to God through Jesus Christ. "Grace and peace be multiplied unto you through the knowledge of God and of Jesus our Lord."[3]

When dissecting Philippians 4:6–7, one should understand the circumstances that surrounded Paul. He was under house arrest. He had external pressures and internal problems, yet he tells us not to be anxious, but give it all up to God. We are to pray, ask, and give thanks for what God has already done. Understand that God does not promise to change our situation, but he does promise to give us peace in any situation. How sweet it is when we look at every trial as a challenge, every precarious circumstance as an opportunity, every difficulty and every tribulation as a chance to rest in the arms of Jesus.

> Come to me ye that labor and are heavy laden and I will give you rest. Take my yoke upon you and learn of me, for I am meek and lowly in heart, and ye shall find rest.[4]

> Peace I leave with you, my peace I give unto you … Let not your heart be troubled, neither let it be afraid.[5]

Philippians 4:6 is a model prayer when we are anxious and worried, for God's peace is promised to guard those who pray with thanksgiving, and that peace will transcend our ability to understand it. The average person fears death, but so often we see the person with a terminal illness find inner peace that is available to all of us, and he or she provides us with a personal testimony to the power of God's peace. Many of God's gifts are not fully comprehensible to us, but when one becomes thankful in every circumstance, one is given a supernatural peace. There is an inner calm because you are dominated by God's peace. Finally, when we rest knowing that he loves us and that "all things work together for good to them that love God,"[6] God's peace is then our peace.

One example that so applies to us and the storms of life we face is Jesus calming the storm. Amid a violent storm on the sea of Galilee, a storm that his disciples were sure would lead to tragedy and certain death, Jesus lay sleeping. The panic of the disciples is seen in that, "His disciples came to him, and awoke him saying, Lord, save us: we perish."[7] Jesus responded,

"Why are you fearful, o you of little faith. Then he arose rebuked the winds and the sea, and there was a great calm."[8] Jesus can calm your storms, and he can smooth your seas. Tranquility can be found in the arms of the Master.

So, peace is not the absence of trouble but the presence of God. It is a fruit of the spirit when God comes to live inside of you. When David was running from King Saul and when King David faced rebellion from Absalom, he was still able to find rest in the Lord: "In peace I will both lie down and sleep, for thou Lord only makest me dwell in safety."[9]

I love artwork; some paintings just jump out and grab me. I am fascinated by how people interpret paintings; what can mean something to you means something different to me. For example, we have two paintings that reflect perfect peace. One painting showed a clear blue mountain lake, calm and serene, surrounded by snow-capped mountains under a beautiful blue sky—definitely a scene that brings a sense of calm. The second painting showed a rugged mountain, a violent, angry storm with lightning and torrential rains that caused a rushing waterfall to cascade down the mountain, yet behind the waterfall in the cleft of a rock lay a tiny bird's nest with a mother protecting her young, who lay safely under her wing. Which painting would you choose? Either shows an example of peace. One shows calm and tranquility, but is that real peace? Peace does not necessarily mean to be in a place without noise, trouble, or hard work. Peace means to be amid noise and trouble and still find calm in your heart. That is real peace.

Inner peace is obviously one of the greatest gifts we can possess. Some people call it happiness, and some call it joy, but it is something more all-encompassing than that. It is a wholeness that suggests completeness, health, justice, prosperity, and protection. It comes from faith in God— who alone embodies all the characteristics of peace. Peace with God leads to peace of mind and peace with others. When we rest in God's sovereignty, we receive a deep and lasting inner peace. This offers us some great advantages. It gives us confident assurance in any circumstance. There is no need to fear the present or the future. Peace calms any internal conflict such as doubt and uncertainty. It gives us comfort and rest. Inner peace allows us to keep things in proper perspective and to interact with those around us in accordance with our wholeness of mind. It brings us true joy and happiness. This happens by "casting all your care upon Him for He careth for you."[10] The fact that we can have wholeness of mind and spirit, the fact that we have a whole heart at rest has little to do with our external surroundings. "Yea, though I walk through the valley of the shadow of death, I will fear no evil; for though art with me; thy rod and thy staff they comfort me."[11]

The peace that we seek is available when we reconcile ourselves with God. We trust that he will do what he says. It is a byproduct of obedience—of following his will. It is a byproduct of dependence on God, that he will take care of our every need.

Back to where I began this chapter, will we ever achieve world peace? Adam and Eve disobeyed God, and Cain killed Able. There seems to have always been conflict since sin came into the world, and the cost of that decision to disobey God has resonated through the centuries. Croesus, the last king of Lydia in 546 BC, gives us the brutal reality of peace and war. "In peace sons bury their fathers, but in war fathers bury their sons."

However, we can find inner peace, and in so doing, we are instructed to share that peace with others. When you make peace with yourself, you can be at peace with the rest of the world. When the mind is calm, its peace is automatically transmitted to everything and everyone. When you focus on changing and calming your inner world, you have more control over your life and can influence those around you.

The blueprint for sharing that peace is found in the following scripture: "Do not repay anyone evil for evil. Be careful to do what is right in the eyes of everyone. If it is possible as far as it depends on you, live at peace with everyone.

> Avenge not yourselves, but rather give place unto wrath, for it is written, vengeance is mine; I will repay, saith the Lord. … if thine enemy hunger, feed him; if he thirst, give him drink … overcome evil with good.[12]

> Follow peace with all men.[13]

> If it be possible, much as lieth in you, live peaceably with all men.[14]

The word *peace* is mentioned 429 times in the Bible. There is a reason. God wants us to have inner peace. God wants the world to live in peace. Living life to the fullest means being at peace. "These things I have spoken unto you, that in me ye might have peace. In the world ye shall have tribulation: but be of good cheer; I have overcome the world."[15] By trusting in his Word, by being obedient to his commands, by depending on him to shelter you during the storm, "You will go out in joy and be led forth in peace; the mountains and hills shall break forth before you into singing, and all the trees of the field shall clap their hands"[16] "Now the God of hope fill you with joy and peace in believing, that ye may abound in hope."[17]

The coming of Christ was ushered in with the phrase "on earth peace, good will toward men."[18] It is through him that we can find inner peace and the world can achieve world peace.

Shalom, and peace be with you, the peace of God that transcends our understanding.

WISDOM

The fear of the Lord is the beginning of Wisdom.
—Proverbs 9:10, Psalm 111:10

Solomon and Bunk King were two men born three thousand years apart, yet both were blessed with one of God's greatest gifts—wisdom. Solomon has often been called the wisest man who ever lived, but in the eyes of a teenage boy, Bunk King certainly was a close second. As my grandfather reached the end of his days on this earth, he did so with grace, peace, and, yes, a bit of humor. In those last days he reminded me that though his body was weakening, his mind was strong, and if I overheard him talking to himself, I was not to worry, as "he always liked to talk to a wise man, and he liked to listen to a wise man talk."

What did these two wise men have in common? They understood that "the fear of the Lord is the beginning of wisdom." Solomon as king could have asked for anything, but what he asked for was wisdom. "Give your servant an understanding heart to judge your people, that I may discern between 'good and bad.'"[1] God's infinite wisdom is shown by the following response: "Because thou asked for wisdom and not for a long life, nor riches, nor the death of your enemies, I have given you that which you have not asked, both riches and honor."[2]

What is wisdom—humanity's wisdom and God's wisdom? Though related, a difference exists. First look at wisdom as defined by humankind. Wisdom is intelligence, knowledge, and understanding with the ability to use these to think an act in such a way that common sense prevails, and choices are beneficial and productive. Wisdom entails the skillfulness to formulate a plan and carry it out in the best and most effective way. It is the ability to think and act using knowledge, experience, understanding, common sense, and insight in a mature and utilitarian manner. This is the essence of wisdom in humanity's eyes.

God's wisdom represents an entirely different type of wisdom—one that we are to seek but never totally achieve or understand.

> For my thoughts are not your thoughts, neither are your ways my ways, declares the Lord. For the heavens are higher than the earth, ... and my thoughts than your thoughts.[3]

> His understanding is infinite.[4]

God is the source of wisdom. "For the Lord gives wisdom, from his mouth comes knowledge and understanding."[5] It is God's omniscience that undergirds his wisdom.

God's wisdom is conceived as pure, loving, and righteous. It has the power to see and choose the best and highest goal and the surest means of attaining it. Wisdom is the practical side of moral goodness that is only found in the fullness of God. We marvel at a wise man; how much more we should marvel at the wisdom of God. "The wisdom that is from above is first pure, then peaceable, gentle, and easy to be entreated, full of mercy and good fruits, without partiality and without hypocrisy."[6] Belief in God ascribes to him perfection and goodness, and as such, he will always pursue the course that is wisest and best.

Biblical wisdom operates on two levels—reflective wisdom that provides answers on the meaning of life, and practical wisdom that provides answers on the issues of life such as industry, integrity, family, and so much more. The books of Job, Ecclesiastes, Proverbs, and some of the Psalms are often referred to as the wisdom books and provide us with perfect guidelines on living life.

Of course, Jesus represents God's ultimate manifestation of wisdom. We first see that on display when as a boy of twelve he made that wisdom apparent as he talked to the scribes and Pharisees in the temple. They were astonished at his knowledge and wisdom. "Jesus increased in wisdom and stature, and in favor with God and man."[7]

Godly wisdom is most apparent in the Sermon on the Mount. Those three chapters in Matthew provide us with the proper foundation for successful living. His story of the wise and foolish builder near the end of that sermon gives us insight into God's wisdom. "Whosoever hears these sayings of mine, and doeth them, I will liken him unto a wise man, which built his house upon a rock. And the rain descended, and the floods came, and the winds blew, and beat upon that house, and it fell not: for it was founded upon a rock. And everyone that heareth these sayings of mine, and doeth them not, shall be like a foolish man, which built his house upon the sand, and the rain descended and the winds blew, and beat upon that house, and it fell, and great was the fall of it."[8] The storms of life are real, but the wise man establishes a firm foundation to help him withstand the storms of life. My favorite line in any song is one penned by Bob Dylan in "Forever Young": "May you have a strong foundation when the wind of changes shift." Biblical wisdom provides such a foundation.

Most of us struggle with pride, and again the wisdom that Jesus provides gives us insight into godly wisdom. "When someone invites you to a dinner, don't take the place of honor. Someone more important than you might have been invited by the host. Then you are called out in front of everyone that you are in the wrong place, and red faced you will have to make your way to the only place left. Rather, when you are invited to dinner, go and sit in the last place. Then when the host comes, he may very well say 'Friend, come up to the front.' That will give the dinner guests something to talk about. If your nose is in the air, you are going to end up flat on your face. But if you are content to be simply yourself, you will become more than yourself."[9] This wisdom offered by God gives us practical answers and advice for Christian living.

There is no better place to go for this advice than the book of James. It not only helps answer the philosophical questions of life but also gives us keen insight into life and the ways of dealing with life's problems. "If any of you lack wisdom, you should ask God, that giveth to all men liberally, and upbraideth not, and it shall be given to him."[10]

This verse tells us how to tap into God's wisdom; simply ask for it. The Bible repeats this simple truth repeatedly.

> Give me understanding that I may learn your commandments.[11]

> For God giveth to a man that is good in his sight wisdom,
> and knowledge and joy: but to the sinner he giveth travail,
> together and the heap up, that he may give to him that is
> good before God.[12]

We must first want wisdom, and in so doing we find the path to wisdom. The place to start is in prayer asking God to grant you wisdom.

I have known a lot of smart people. The knowledge found in books does not make you wise. So, what is the difference between knowledge and wisdom? Jimi Hendrix had a gift, and that was playing a guitar like no other human on the planet. One might feel cheated that his life was tragically cut short; however, he did leave us a valuable clue into the difference between knowledge and wisdom in one simple statement: "Knowledge speaks, but wisdom listens." What are some other clues that allow us to separate knowledge and wisdom?

From the philosophers of Greece to the scientists of today, they discovered that wisdom was not found in books but in a lifetime of attempting to find the truth—to find wisdom. Immanuel Kant said, "Science is organized knowledge, wisdom is organized life." Charles Spurgeon said, "Wisdom is the right use of knowledge, but to know is not to be wise. Many men know a great deal, and are the greater fools for it. There is no fool so great a fool as a knowing fool, but knowing how to use knowledge is to have wisdom." One thing we learn is that abundance of knowledge does not teach men to be wise, that indeed, these two enviable qualities are separate, distant virtues. Leo Tolstoy, the great Russian writer, said that "real wisdom is not the knowledge of everything, but the knowledge of which things in life are necessary, which are less necessary, and which are completely unnecessary to know." Perhaps the saddest indictment of our society today is that we gather knowledge faster than we gather wisdom.

How do we get wisdom? Again, I go to the Bible for advice. First, we must want it; we must seek it.

> The heart of the prudent getteth knowledge and the ear
> of the wise seeketh knowledge.[13]

Counsel in the heart of man is like deep water, but a man
of understanding will draw it out.[14]

Second, we are to surround ourselves with others who seek wisdom.

He that walketh with wise men shall be wise.[15]

A scorner loveth not one that reproveth him: neither will
he go unto the wise.[16]

Unfortunately, a third way we gain wisdom is through experience. Experience can be a tough teacher, but if our goal is to gain wisdom, experience can serve us well. We will not find wisdom in a textbook. You cannot get knowledge enough to make you wise. You cannot get it simply from hearing it from others. Oftentimes experience is the best teacher and is a valuable tool in gaining wisdom. I am reminded of the humor of Will Rogers: "Good judgment comes from experience, and a lot of that comes from bad judgment." Samuel Smiles, the Scottish author and reformer, said, "Wisdom and understanding become the possession of individual men by travelling the old road of observation, attention, preference, and industry." The experience gathered from books, though valuable, is but the nature of learning; whereas the experience gained from actual life is the nature of wisdom. Herb Caen may say it best: "A man begins cutting his wisdom teeth the first time he bites off more than he can chew."

I am reminded of the story of two lumberjacks involved in a competition to see who could cut down the most trees during an eight-hour contest. One lumberjack was young and extraordinarily strong with energy to burn. The second lumberjack was old and gray with many years of experience. The young man worked all day, never taking a break and seemingly never running out of energy. Occasionally he would stop just for a second, and to his surprise, he would not hear the noise of the saw of the old lumberjack. At the end of the day, the young man was confident of victory only to be disappointed. The old man had taken down almost twice as many trees. When asked how he did it, he simply smiled and said, "I stopped every hour and sharpened my blades."

We can learn and gain wisdom from experience, which is why we need to value people like Bunk King. It was his age and the experiences of his life that so revered him to me. Most societies treat elders with great respect. They seem to realize their value to their family and to society as a whole. The Bible is full of examples of God using older people for his purpose. Moses was eighty years old before he was ready to be used by God.

Job 12:12 says it best: "With the ancient is wisdom; and in length of days understanding." Japanese society reveres the older members of their society and encourages ancestor worship. The wisdom and experience of older people is a great resource that we should not take lightly. Our society is much the better when we recognize the contributions of older people. We need only to look at the political climate in the United States, where both of our current political parties are led by men in their seventies.

We all wish to have value in our lives—to be valuable to our family and our society—and we should reflect that, whether we are twenty-seven or eighty-seven. We have much to learn from the elderly, even their approach of death. Jean de la Fontaine, a French poet of the seventeenth century, said, "Death never takes the wise man by surprise, he is always ready to go." Leonardo da Vinci echoes that sentiment: "As a well spent day brings happy sleep, so a life well spent brings happy death." In my seventieth year of life, it is my desire to continue to gain wisdom and to continue to add value to those around me.

What is the value of wisdom and what are the benefits? The Bible continually tells us that wisdom is better than wealth.

> How much better is it to get wisdom than gold to gain understanding rather than silver.[18]

> As an earring of gold, and an ornament of fine gold, so is a wise reprover upon an obedient ear.[19]

> Forsake her not and she shall preserve thee; love her and she shall keep thee. Wisdom is the principle thing, therefore get wisdom, and with all thy getting get understanding.[20]

> He who walks in wisdom will be delivered.[21]

Buy the truth and sell it not; also wisdom, instruction, and understanding.[22]

We must realize that wisdom, understanding, and knowledge are gifts of the Holy Spirit and are more valuable than silver, gold, diamonds, platinum, or whatever this world has to offer.

King Solomon, the wisest man who ever lived, writes in a message that reflects the gift God had given him. I can picture him reflecting near the end of his life about wisdom, and wealth as he writes, "A man's wisdom maketh his face to shine." 23 The great philosopher Sophocles said, "Wisdom outweighs any wealth." It has been my experience that as you attempt to walk in the divine wisdom of God, you see victory and success in your life.

In our search for wisdom, we must be aware that the journey never ends. Benjamin Franklin once said that "the doors of wisdom are never shut." In seeking wisdom, we are wise; in believing that we have attained it, we are foolish. To continue our growth, we must continue to seek, and we must continue to question.

Finally, in our search for wisdom, we must also look for a way to assist those around us with what we have learned. Epicuras once said, "Of all things which wisdom provides to make life entirely happy, much the greatest is the possession of friendship." A wise man understands the value of friendship. One of my worst mistakes in life was not understanding the importance of friendship, and it haunts me to this day. Duke was my best friend from first grade to sixth grade. We shared everything. Either he was at my house, or I was at his. We played army, we were cowboys, we went fishing, and we went swimming. You get the picture; this was a special friend. Then came junior high, a larger school with new friends to make. The problem was that my set of new friends did not accept Duke. He wasn't cool enough to run with us. So, I turned my back on a friend—a true friend that would have been by my side to face any battle. Years went by, and I simply but ignorantly devalued that friendship. It has since come back to haunt me as I wisely learned that real relationships are hard to come by and should always be protected. For there is no point of having wisdom if you cannot share its benefits with others. A wise man will nurture his relationships and in so doing will not only bring benefits to others but benefits to himself.

In our world today we need wise people willing to share their wisdom with others. And where does wisdom start? "The fear of the Lord is the beginning of wisdom." When we seek wisdom, God is more than willing to provide the avenues to achieve what is indeed one of God's greatest gifts—wisdom.

ENDURANCE

I have fought a good fight, I have finished
my course, I have kept the faith.

—2 Timothy 4:7

This is the verse, above all other verses, that I want to repeat at the end of my life. As one pauses to dissect this specific verse, all of life's meaning and purpose is clarified. "I have fought a good fight," though we have gone through tough times, we proved tougher; though we have been knocked down, we always got back up; and though we have gone through the storms of life, they have always given way to the sun. "I have finished my course," speaks to the purpose we have all been blessed. The goal is not to start the race but to finish the race. "I have kept the faith," speaks to our values—our ability to be true to our beliefs and not compromise that belief system.

It is all about endurance. It is about the ability of one to go through the wear and tear and still complete the task at hand. It is about the ability to overcome challenges, push through, and come out victorious. It is about the ability to withstand hardship and adversity. It is about the ability to sustain a prolonged stressful effort or activity. It is that ability to push through the pain when your heart has been broken, when you have lost your job, and when everything that could go wrong did go wrong, but you had the ability to endure.

We often think of endurance when it comes to that gifted athlete. In today's world of sport, we look at Tom Brady at forty-two still performing on a football field at the highest level with people fifteen and twenty years younger. We look at LeBron James who after seventeen years in the National Basketball Association had perhaps his finest season. The endurance of these great athletes did not just happen. It took commitment on their part to succeed and to overcome what hardships were placed in their path.

The journey of life has often been compared to a marathon, and there are certainly lessons to be learned and applied as one trains for a marathon that fit the race of life. The first step in preparation for a marathon is commitment and self-discipline. If we are to be successful in life, those two qualities are essential. We can want to be successful at something, but to achieve it takes a commitment and the self-discipline to make it happen. A favorite phrase of mine is, "Success is spelled W-O-R-K."

Second, you must lay aside every weight. When a marathoner runs his race, that person does not run with a backpack or a coat; rather he finds the lightest of shoes and clothes so as not to be encumbered. I am reminded of the ancient Greeks who ran their races at Mount Olympus in the nude so as not to be loaded down with unnecessary baggage. We are not to let the worries of life, the complexities of life, and, yes, the temptations of life slow us down or derail our purpose, goals, and objectives. "No temptations or burden has overtaken you that is not common to mankind. And God is faithful. He will not let you be tempted beyond what you can bear. But when you are tempted, he will also provide a way out so that you can endure it."[1]

Third, we are to run with endurance. The marathon starts with a single step, and training for a marathon begins with a plan, a commitment, and self-discipline. Most of the training books I have seen suggest anywhere from twelve to sixteen weeks are necessary to be ready to successfully complete a marathon. The race of life requires endurance if we are to successfully complete our journey.

Fourth, we must set the right pace. In a tribute to Marilyn Monroe, Elton John speaks of her candle burning out much too quickly. Be it actors like John Belushi or singers like Jimi Hendrix, life's pace can go at warp speed. The marathon runner knows that the right pace is essential in running the successful race, and we must set the right pace as we approach life.

A fifth thing the marathoner must do is mentally prepare for the hills. The marathoner examines the course he is to run and trains for the hills that he will encounter, and though physically ready, one must also prepare mentally for that part of the race. The same is true with life. We know there will be hills to climb; we know there will be wind and rain and storms that make us want to stop and quit the course, but there are verses that give us hope.

Let us run with patience the race that is set before us.[2]

We also glory in our sufferings, knowing that suffering produces perseverance, perseverance produces character, and character hope.[3]

What happens when you hit the wall, when you have to run twenty miles, and it seems you have nothing left to give, but somehow, some way your character kicks in; you will finish the race, and you will achieve your goal. What happens when you hit the wall in life? May I suggest prayer. God does not forget our labor of love. He will not forget us, and he will not give up on us. God is ready and willing to help us and provide us strength and endurance. "I can do all things through Christ who strengthens me."[4]

Finally, the successful marathoner refocuses on the goal. He sees the finish line, and his body is filled with a new energy of finishing a race, completing the course, realizing that the commitment and discipline necessary to achieve victory have allowed him to fulfill a dream. We do not know the finish line of life, but we need to prepare and focus on finishing the race.

Do you not know that in a race all the runners run, but only one receives the prize?

Run in such a way as to get the prize.[5]

Let us not be weary in well doing, for in due season we shall reap, if we faint not.[6]

There have been many amazing stories surrounding the marathon. Two particularly bear repeating. In 1960 Abebe Bikila won the Olympic marathon held in Rome. Four years later, in 1964, he would be back to claim the gold in Tokyo. Back-to-back Olympic victories in the marathon was no small feat, but his second victory came forty days after an appendicitis attack. What a remarkable testament to overcoming adversity to claim the prize!

This was followed by an even more intriguing human life story in the 1968 Olympics held in Mexico City. In that race John Stephen Akhwari of Tanzania stumbled and fell, severely hurting his knee and ankle. By 7:00 p.m. an Ethiopian runner had crossed the finish line to win the gold medal. Over the next hour all other racers made their way across the finish line, and a mostly empty stadium witnessed the triumph of human will. Limping through the stadium gates came Akhwari with his leg heavily wrapped. When asked why he continued, he responded, "My country did not send me seven thousand miles to begin a race; they sent me to finish the race." Endurance and strength come from many sources, and we should never underestimate the power of the human spirit.

How does one become a champion on the sports field, in the classroom, on the job, or, in a general sense, in life itself?

Here are ten things that I believe champions seem to have in common:

- They get comfortable being uncomfortable.
- They don't just do their best; they do whatever it takes.
- They push their limits and redefine their goals.
- They think about what the competition is doing, and they do more.
- They see mistakes and defeats as opportunities for growth.
- They believe that they will succeed and that faith in success is greater their fear of failure.
- They work on strengthening their shortcomings.
- They view hard work as a challenge and as an opportunity—a stepping stone to achieving their goals.
- They endure by going a little harder, running a little faster, and making the extra sacrifice.
- They know that ultimate success comes through the accumulation of small victories. There are many keys to becoming a champion in life, but the list above puts you well on your way.

Like most things in life, we can learn valuable life lessons in the scriptures, and no one individual teaches us more about endurance than

Job. Here was a man of great wealth that lived some four thousand years ago. The scriptures say that he had "7000 head of sheep, 3000 camels, 500 team of oxen, 500 donkeys, and a large number of servants."[7]

He was also blessed with seven sons and three daughters. Life was good for Job. He was honest and totally devoted to God, and then tragedy struck. A tribe of Sabeans stole his animals and killed all but one of his field hands. A bolt of lightning struck the sheep and killed the shepherds. Chaldeans raided the camels and massacred the camel drivers. His children, while attending a party, were struck by a tornado, and all were killed. Yet with all these calamities, Job endured and praised his God. "Naked I came from my mother's womb, and naked I will depart. The lord gave and the Lord has taken away, may the name of the Lord be praised."[8]

His suffering was only increased by failing health. Job was struck with terrible sores from head to foot. Job's wife said that he should even curse God and die, yet Job endured. Three of Job's friends came to offer their advice, but their words rang hollow as Job continued his suffering. Though he questioned God for his suffering, he continued to praise God. "With Him is wisdom and strength, He hath counsel and understanding."[9]

Through it all Job endured, and ultimately God spoke to Job and blessed Job's later life even more than his earlier life. He ended up with "14,000 sheep, 6000 camels, 1000 yoke of oxen, and 1000 donkeys. He also had seven sons and three daughters."[10] It is said that Job lived another 140 years, living to see his children and grandchildren.

Job's name is synonymous with suffering and endurance. The suffering that he experienced is the same that we suffer—the loss of family, wealth, personal health, and personal relationships. Yet Job did not curse God; he questioned God, and at times cried out that he wished he had not been born. One of the great lessons found in the book of Job is the dignity found in suffering, and the ultimate realization that God is present in our suffering. Shared suffering and great endurance can be dignifying and life changing. God sees our suffering and shares our pain.

This leads us to God's endurance.

The goodness of God endureth continually.[11]

The Lord is good, his mercy is everlasting, and his truth endureth to all generations.[12]

Thy mercy O Lord endureth forever.[13]

The word of the Lord endureth forever.[14]

Goodness, mercy, truth—these words all define God's endurance.

God also provides us with the ability to endure. God provides us with hope, patience, and endurance to deal with whatever life throws at us.

Being strengthened with all power according to His glorious might that you may have great endurance and patience.[15]

Consider it pure joy, my brothers and sisters, whenever you face trials of many kinds, because you know that the testing of your faith produces endurance.[16]

You need to persevere so that when you have done the will of God, you will receive what he has promised.[17]

Blessed is the man that endureth temptation, for when he is tried, he shall receive the crown of life, which the Lord hath promise to them that love Him.[18]

The richness of God's Word provides us with the answers we need when trials arise and when suffering occurs. When you struggle to endure, let God provide you the strength to carry on. "Fix your eyes on Jesus, the pioneer and perfector of faith. For the joy set before Him he endured the cross, scorning its shame, and sat down at the right hand of the throne of God."[19]

The lesson of endurance is a valuable one that leads to success. Whether it is the champion on the sports field that simply outworks everyone to achieve greatness or the person who struggles with a health issue, there is a moment when you find inner strength that I believe is the presence of God rewarding your patience and endurance. We are told: "Keep your head in all situations, endure hardship … discharge all duties." 20

Franklin Roosevelt, one of America's greatest presidents, and one who was well aware of pain and suffering, gives us a great quote: "When you get to the end of your rope, tie a knot in it and hang on." The great boxer Jack Dempsey said, "A champion is someone who gets up even when he can't." By never giving up, by managing to endure, we have taken the steps necessary to succeed. We have fought the good fight, we have finished the race, and we have kept the faith.

HUMILITY

What doth The Lord require of thee? To do justly, to
love mercy, and to walk humbly with thy God.

—Micah 6:8

These are three requirements that touch the very core of the Christian faith. Each carries with it a message of importance to mankind. First, we are to be fair and just toward one another. Second, we are to have a compassion for one another that goes beyond fairness, a kindness in excess that allows us to forgive when forgiveness is not warranted. Third, we are to walk humbly with God. It is the third part of this holy scripture that I want to examine. What does it mean to walk humbly with God?

Webster defines the word *humble* as not proud, not self-assertive and modest; showing a consciousness of one's defects or shortcomings; lowly, unpretentious; to be lower in condition or rank; modest, lowly, meek; a mildness and patience of disposition not easily stirred to anger or resentment.

In our world today, we often view greatness in terms of power, possession, prestige, and position. There seems to be a me first mentality with no room for humility. Yet the Lord makes it clear that being humble is a requirement that we as Christians are to have.

What does Christian humility entail? First and foremost, it entails service. In service to others we find obedience to the Lord. The best example of this service in obedience was Jesus. "And being found in fashion as a man, he humbled himself, and became obedient unto death, even the death of the cross."[1] Jesus referred to himself as a humble servant. Think of it; Jesus washed feet, helped children, fixed breakfast, and served lepers. He came to serve, and it was because of his greatness that he did these things.

John 13:1–17 reveals the story of Jesus washing the feet of his disciples. This was a great teaching moment. The custom of that time was for the lowliest servant to perform this distasteful duty of washing the dirty, filthy feet of strangers or travelers before they entered the house. Yet here was Jesus doing something that only a lowly servant would do. It also reveals the mark of a great leader—a willingness to do any task. He would not ask us to do something he would not do. No task was beneath Jesus because he had a servant's heart. You will never arrive at a place in life where you are too important to help with menial tasks.

We serve God by humbling ourselves and serving others. Along with service comes obedience. We cannot pick and choose who we are to serve and when we are to obey. We are to serve where we are needed.

One of the great humanitarians of the twentieth century was Mother Teresa. She represents a perfect example of humbly walking with God. At nineteen years of age, this young girl from Albania became a nun and followed the Lord's call to Dublin, Ireland, where she joined the Sisters of Loreto. One year later she was on her way to India to teach the poor of Calcutta. On September 10, 1946, sister Mary Therese received her "call within a call" to leave the order and work with the poor and sick of Calcutta, India. Her goal—her call—was to "aid the unwanted, the unloved, the uncared for." Servants, and those rare people who define true humility, think more about others than themselves.

Mother Theresa would first begin an open-air school and a home for the dying destitute. This would lead to her opening a colony for lepers, an orphanage, a nursing home, family clinics, and mobile health clinics. Her work became international by opening clinics in New York City in 1971. Her organization, Missionaries of Charity, ultimately expanded to 610 foundations in 123 countries. She was awarded the Jewel of India for her service, and in 1979 she was awarded the Nobel Peace Prize for "bringing help to suffering humanity."

Mother Teresa was beatified by the Catholic Church. By her church she is considered a saint, and by the world she is considered one of the greatest humanitarians and the most recognizable woman of the twentieth century. How did she become such a revered figure? It was because she did not judge people; she merely loved them. It was because she did whatever it took to get the job done. It was because she valued all human life. Finally, it was because her example was Jesus, and her calling was the world.

The examples of Jesus Christ and Mother Theresa reveal a special truth about those who humble themselves into obedience to God. They will be exalted. God measures greatness in terms of service not status. "God resisteth the proud, and giveth grace to the humble. Humble yourselves therefore under the mighty hand of God, that he may exalt you in due time."[2] Three times are the following words repeated in the gospels: "He that shall humble himself shall be exalted."[3] "Humble yourselves in the sight of the Lord, and he shall lift you up."[4] It is clear to me that the Lord has a special heart for the humble.

One of the real ironies lies in the following scripture: "Blessed are the meek, for they shall inherit the earth."[5] Think of those people who reflect a character opposite of humility—one of arrogance, pride, and haughtiness. Do we really enjoy those people? Do we enjoy people who always talk and never listen?

Do we appreciate one who rejects advice and refuses to accept help? How do we argue with someone who stubbornly refuses to change his or her mind when that person knows he or she is wrong? Do we like to be around someone who sees everything through self? Arrogance and selfishness are divisive. Obsession with self that excludes others hurts everyone. "For where envying and strife is, there is confusion and every evil work."[6]

So, what are we to do? We are to seek wisdom and the honor one will find by walking humbly with the Lord. Paul speaks to this in his letter to the Philippians.

> Let nothing be done through strife or vainglory; but in lowliness of mind let each esteem others better themselves. Look not every man on his own things, but every man on the things of others.[7]

> When pride cometh, then cometh shame; but with the lowly is wisdom.[8]

Before destruction the heart of a man is haughty, and before honor is humility.[9]

A man's pride shall bring him low; but honor shall uphold the humble in spirit.[10]

By humility and the fear of the Lord are riches, and honor, and life.[11]

In the eyes of God, a humble person is considered wise; he is honored, is given life, and is exalted.

We have seen that humility entails service and obedience, but what else is involved? The Bible says that we are to "walk … with all lowliness and meekness, with long-suffering, forbearing one another in love."[12] We are to "put on … mercy, kindness, humbleness of mind, meekness, and long-suffering."[13] Christian humility is the grace that makes one think of himself no more highly then he ought to think. In honor, we prefer our brethren to ourselves. It does not demand undo self-depreciation or lowering the view of oneself but freedom from vanity.

Are we not all the same in the eyes of God? There are no great or nongreat people. The difference is our values. Great values deliver great character, and humility is a great value. I am reminded of a story by Benjamin Franklin when asked the definition of a gentleman. A gentleman, Franklin responded, was one "who could get down on his hands and knees and scrub the floors with a cleaning lady or eat dinner with the President of the United States and feel perfectly comfortable doing either."

Let us list some of the attributes of the humble. The humble seek guidance from God and others. "Hear counsel and receive instruction … that thou mayest be wise."[14] The humble will listen to what their critics say. We learn from our sins and our shortcomings and our mistakes, as we turn our stumbling blocks into stepping-stones.

The humble person is honest. Humility is not putting yourself down or denying your strengths; it is being honest about your weaknesses. A humble person says, "I need help; I can't do it alone." In honesty and humility, we draw support to our side. We can be trusted; we are not trying to take all the credit. We share the credit, and when we share the credit, we become more productive and more successful. We are naturally drawn to humble people, as honest, authentic people naturally attract us. Remember that God will use our weaknesses as well as our strengths, and he works best with us when we admit our weaknesses.

Humility is selfless. Humility doesn't make you think less of yourself; it simply makes you think of yourself less. It gives you a heart of service where you not only look out for your own personal interest but also the interest of others. It is important to have a good self-image. Having a strong, clear gaze into ourselves is necessary, but we want to guard our hearts and ensure that we seek the Lord.

As a coach who has worked with young people for forty years, I have learned a few lessons about humility, and they are lessons that you can apply to your life. Growing up, I particularly admired two coaches: John Wooden, the legendary basketball coach at UCLA, and Bud Wilkinson, the legendary football coach at the University of Oklahoma. Both carried themselves modestly. They never sought credit for themselves, and they taught their players the importance of teamwork. They both understood that much could be accomplished by teamwork when no one is concerned about who gets the credit. Charles (Bud) Wilkinson coached the Oklahoma Sooners from 1947 to 1963 and recorded 145 victories. During his tenure, the Sooners had winning streaks of thirty-one and forty-seven games. The string of forty-seven straight victories is still the NCAA record today. Wilkinson had led the Minnesota Gophers to three national champions as a collegiate, and as a coach he won thirteen consecutive conference titles and three national championships. The Sooners went twelve years and seventy-nine consecutive games without a loss in conference play. That is quite a bit to brag about, but as a young boy growing up, what I admired about coach Wilkinson was his soft-spoken approach, his humility, and his willingness to give the credit to the players and the other coaches.

Coach John Wooden is considered by many to be the greatest college basketball coach in the history of the sport. Coach Wooden led the UCLA Bruins for twenty-seven years and compiled a record of 620–147. This included ten national championships and seven consecutive national championships. During those years he amassed two amazing records that may never be surpassed in men's basketball—eighty-eight consecutive wins, and thirty-eight consecutive NCAA tournament wins. Yet what I remember most about John Wooden was his soft-spoken approach, his humility, and his willingness to give the credit to his players and the other coaches.

Both coaching legends understood that when no one is concerned about who gets the credit, much can be accomplished, and that a player who makes the team great is better than a great player. Great players and great coaches deflect glory away from themselves and onto others. Robert Schuller speaks to the principle of positive giving: "Whatever you give away will always come back to you." Coaches Wooden and Wilkinson were team builders; they deflected the credit and became recognized as great for what they accomplished. What they gave to others was returned to them many times over.

Humility is an attractive quality. More importantly, it is a godly quality. It is a quality of the wise: "the meek will He guide in judgment; the meek will he teach his way."[15] Humility is a quality that leads to grace. "God resisteth the proud, but giveth grace unto the humble."[16] Humility is a quality that personifies Jesus. "Take my yoke upon you, and learn from me; for I am meek and humble in heart; and ye shall find rest unto your soul."[17] Humility is a quality that brings salvation: "Receive with meekness the engrafted word which is able to save your souls."[18]

Three things the Lord requires of you are: to be fair and just, to be compassionate and love mercy, and to walk humbly with God. It is not easy to fulfill these requirements, but as you seek the Lord, your help will come.

CONTENTMENT, PEACE, PURPOSE, CONFIDENCE, ABUNDANCE

The Lord is my shepherd, I lack nothing. He makes me lie down in green pastures, he leads me beside quiet waters, he refreshes my soul. He guides me along the right path for his name's sake. Even though I walk through the darkest valley, I will fear no evil, for you are with me; your rod and your staff they comfort me. You prepare a table before me in the presence of my enemies. You anoint my head with oil; my cup overflows. Surely your goodness and mercy will follow me all the days of my life, and I will dwell in the house of the Lord forever.
—Psalm 23 (New International Version)

Wow! This is a song written three thousand years ago that is still as relevant today as it was in ancient times. The reason is simple; written by King David but inspired by the Holy Spirit, it touches the very core of human emotion and what our souls long for.

Bob Marley, the great Rastafarian musician from Jamaica, had three things placed in his casket: his red Les Paul guitar, a stock of Ganga marijuana, and the Bible. The Bible was to be placed on his chest next to his heart and opened to Psalm 23. Now I can't play the guitar, and I've never tried marijuana, but the idea of having a Bible accompany me to my grave and it being open to Psalm 23 is indeed an appealing idea.

There is a reason this is one of the first scriptures children learn, and the one they repeat as they are growing up. There is a reason it continues to stay with us through this life and is on our mind and on our lips as we finish our journey in this life. The reason is simple; it answers our every need. It gives assurance from God that he will take care of us from the beginning of this life to our transition to the next one. It offers up the assurance of nourishment, rest, guidance, protection, comfort, provision, and future prospect. It provides us with contentment, peace, purpose, confidence, and assurance.

This psalm written by David reveals much about the character of the man and his trust in God. A review of David's life offers us a great insight as to how he was able to write such an important piece of literature. This is the man who as a boy slew the giant Goliath and defeated the Philistine army. This is the young man who had to run for his life because of the jealousies of King Saul and Saul's attempts to kill David. Not without sin, this is the man who would become the king but would sin with Bathsheba and place her husband in harm's way in battle yet be restored to God through his mercy. This is the same David who would see his own son turn against him and threaten the kingdom. Through it all, David had come to trust in the Lord and understand that his God was like the shepherd he had been as a boy—a caring shepherd. Our God is one who cares for us, provides food for us, protects and leads us, and finally brings us home safely.

As we mature in our faith, we become more like David. We come to realize what God has done for us. In what years we have left, we continue to expect God to provide for us. We see the God who loves us and who will provide grace for all our needs. We find comfort in joy and in sorrow because the message of this psalm provides us with hope.

"The Lord is my shepherd, I lack nothing." This speaks about our total contentment. David sees God as our shepherd, a good shepherd, one that is going to take care of his sheep. David himself had once risked his life to rescue a lamb. A shepherd makes it his business to protect the flock. God, as the good shepherd, takes us in, protects, and provides for us. Furthermore, it is implied that the good shepherd provides what is in the best interest of his sheep. God will supply us with what we need, not necessarily what we desire, and we may conclude that if it is not given then it is not necessarily good for us, or it is not within God's timing to provide. Because of our trust in God, there's no reason to fear that a need will go unfilled.

Listen to the words of Paul. "I have learned to be content whatever the circumstances … I have learned the secret of being content in any and every situation, whether well fed or hungry, whether living in plenty or in want. I can do all this through him who gives me strength."[1]

Contentment grows out of humility and trusting God. We have become content when we let God have the lead in our lives. Contentment comes out of growing devotion to God. Contentment comes when we care less about the material things in life. It has been said that we should not focus on possessions lest they possess us. Remember that God will supply all your needs, and he will do it in a way that is best for you. When we see life from God's point of view, when we understand that it is not what we have but what we are supposed to do that is important, contentment will become a way of life.

"He makes me lie down in green pastures, he leads me beside quiet waters." Our family loves to go to the mountains. In the winter, we go to ski. The joy and exhilaration of racing down a mountain or breathing the cool, crisp mountain air is simply special. I have seemingly been able to almost touch the beautiful blue sky, and I enjoy seeing the evergreens blanketed with freshly fallen snow. I will make a winter vacation a heavenly experience. The only thing better is a summer vacation in the mountains. The serenity of a clear, calm, blue mountain lake surrounded by a blanket of mountain flowers and green pastures with aspen trees in the background and their leaves gently dancing in the light breeze brings a calmness and a peace that seem to provide a testimony to how great our God is. However, vacations are fleeting. How do we keep the peace? How do we keep that feeling of green pastures and quiet waters?

We need to understand the spiritual nature of this verse. We have the support and comfort of this life provided to us by our shepherd. It is the goodness of God that allows our enjoyment in life, and whether we have been blessed with much or little, it is provided by God and is therefore a green pasture. The Bible itself—the Word of God—provides a spiritual nourishment that allows us to never be on parched, baron ground but to always have green pastures for feeding. The completeness—the wholeness that we feel within our souls—is because God guides us beside quiet waters. We don't just pass through, but we lie down and stay. This is our place of rest.

When we feed on God's goodness, we must follow his direction. That direction will never guide us the wrong way. Because of his love, we will find our thirst quenched and our weariness satisfied with rest. He will always lead us to the quiet waters, not the stagnant waters that gather filth and not the rapid rolling floods that bring danger, but the quiet running waters where we find calmness for our internal conflicts, where fear and doubt are erased by the peace of God. The way to bring peace to a troubled heart is to trust in God's promises and depend on him to do what he said he would do.

"He restoreth my soul." Thank God that he is a God of mercy and love. As David writes this, I see him looking back on past mistakes and transgressions—mistakes that left him in misery, struggling and suffering with no peace of mind. Guilt-ridden, he went to God and poured out his heart and asked forgiveness: "Have mercy on me, oh God, according to your unfailing love, according to your great compassion blot out my transgressions. Wash away all my inequities and cleanse me from my sin."[2] We have all been in that dark place, and that promise we find here in verse 3 is that God will restore our souls. He will bring back peace and joy and can make them effective and a part of his purpose.

"He leadeth me in the paths of righteousness." He does this for his purpose. We want purpose in life; that purpose is to glorify God, to honor him by doing his will, and to serve his purpose. God leads us to the path of righteousness and then continues to lead us on the path. God is willing to recover me when I fall and revive me when I grow weak. I believe that God has a purpose for our lives; he has blueprints already drawn, specifications written out, and a great purpose for us. When I was seventeen, I felt God's call to be a minister, but I rebelled and left the path the Lord wanted for me. After years of wandering, of finding turmoil and heartache in life that I tried to control, I came back in search of those paths of righteousness, and God restored my soul. He closed one door, that of being a minister, and opened another. Essentially God said, "I can't use you as a minister any longer, but if you are willing and obedient, I can use you as a teacher. Teaching at a private Christian school and teaching Sunday school classes in my local church have given me purpose and fulfillment. God truly will restore your soul and lead you along, "The right path for his name's sake." The past is the past, but when you follow God's guidance, you know you are where God wants you. There is a purpose in placing you where you are right now. You can better understand God's purpose for your life by what he wants you to do now.

"Though I walk through the darkest valley, I will fear no evil, for you are with me." The King James version says the "valley of the shadow of death." Either way, David expressed confidence because he knew he was with God. Our confidence grows out of our reliance on God. The story of Gideon's defeat of the Midianites is a great example. Gideon had thirty-two thousand troops at his disposal, but in obedience to God he took only three hundred into battle and let the Lord do the rest. We fall into a trap when we think we can conquer our dark shadows in our own strength. We become more effective when we rely on God. God loves us, God is with us, and when we understand our value to God, we need never fear the difficult trials of life and death. Our faith in God does not make trouble disappear, but it does make the troubles something we can face with confidence and without fear.

God not only leads us through the valleys; he comforts us by his Word and his Spirit. In times like this he will comfort us. That confidence was expressed boldly by the prophet Isaiah, "Fear not, for I have redeemed thee, I have called thee by thy name; thou art mine. When thou passeth through the waters, I will be with thee, and through the rivers, they shall not overflow thee. When thou walkest through the fire, thou shalt not be burned ... For I am the Lord your God."[3] We can always have the assurance and confidence to know that our God is always present in the good times and in the dark shadows of the valleys of life.

"You prepare a table before me ... my cup overflows." The Lord has provided me all that I need both physically and spiritually—everything I need for body and soul. God prepares the table, and he spares no expense. Not only does he provide for my needs, but he provides even more— plentiful provisions for the life we have now and the one that is to come. Jesus Christ gives us these words, "I have come that they may have life, and have it to the full."[4] God is the giver of every good and perfect gift, and he willingly provides it all for you and me.

"Surely goodness and mercy will follow me all the days of my life."

David's life had given him the confidence that God would always provide. God's never-ending mercy had provided him pardoning love, protecting love, sustaining love, and continual love. There is no reason to believe that God's goodness and mercy will stop. It will continue all the days of our lives. For whom God loves he loves to the end. Once we are a child of God, he will never leave us or forsake us.

"I will dwell in the house of the Lord forever." David introduced something new in this last statement—hope in a future beyond this life. Pleased with what God has done in his life, he looks forward to much more in the house of the Lord. David, through the leadership of the Holy Spirit, declares that there would be a celestial home at the end of life's journey. That confidence, that assurance, was built through a lifetime of allowing God to guide and direct him, by being obedient to his call, and by placing his trust and faith in him. We can find the same contentment, the same peace, the same purpose, the same confidence, and the same abundance in life through simply believing in who God is and allowing him to do in our lives what he purposes to do.

GIVING

For God so loved the world that he gave his only begotten Son, that whosoever believeth in him should not perish but have everlasting life.
—John 3:16

"So loved … that he gave" allows us to first understand that giving is done out of love. God so loved that he gave: "He did not spare his own son, but gave him up for us all. How will he not also, along with him graciously give us all things."[1] There is a special comfort in knowing the love realized at the cross. With God, he provided the greatest gift with the greatest love.

To understand the benefits of giving, we must understand the divine character of God and the promises that God makes to us about giving. Our God is a giving God, and giving expresses his righteousness. Giving to us is an integral part of his character. When we are weary, he gives us rest. When you need guidance and wisdom, "you should ask of God, who gives generously to all without finding fault, and it will be given to you."[2] When you need peace, "my peace I give you."[3] The psalmist says, "Delight thyself also in the Lord, and he shall give thee the desires of thine heart."[4]

Understand that God gives generously and perfectly. "Every good and every perfect gift is from above."[5] Giving is a natural response of love. When you love someone, you want to give time and attention, and provide for his or her total needs. God did this for his son. "For God so loved the world he gave" is one of the more profound statements ever recorded. It speaks of the sacrificial giving offered by Christ, who gave up his rights as God. He gave up his glory out of love and obedience to the Father's will. Christ became poor to allow us to become rich by giving us the offering of salvation and eternal life.

The gift of God is eternal life in Jesus Christ our Lord.[6]

It is by grace you have been saved, through faith, and this is not from yourselves, it is the gift of God.[7]

Thanks be to God for his unspakable gift.[8]

God gives to us so that we can give to others. It is important for us to understand that the purpose of our giving is to honor and bring glory to God. "Whatever you eat or drink or whatever you do, do it all for the glory of God."[9] "Others will praise God … for your generosity in sharing with them and with everyone else."[10] That is why a prerequisite for giving is to first give ourselves to the Lord's service. He is not interested in your gifts until he has you.

The Lord expects us and requires us to give. Certain commands throughout the Bible make this clear.

Give to the one who ask you, and do not turn away from the one who wants to borrow from you.[11]

Every man shall give as he is able, according to the blessing of the Lord thy God which he hath given thee.[12]

The righteous giveth and spareth not.[13]

He answereth and sayeth to them, he that hath two coats led him impart to him that hath none, and he that hath meat led him do likewise.[14]

When I was a kid, I eagerly anticipated Christmas. The idea that it was more blessed to give than to receive made me question whether all the Bible could possibly be true. I still look forward to Christmas, but it is the giving that has become the blessing for me, and the notion that in giving there is a real blessing has become a reality.

An experience I had some twenty years ago brings the biblical truth to the forefront. I was checking in some rental equipment at the local bus depot; yes that's right, in a small town sometimes businesses wear two hats. A young man was just getting off the bus and asked me for directions to the Salvation Army. He looked tired and hungry, so instead of giving him walking directions, I loaded him up in my car. That was the first nudge God gave me. The second nudge was sharing a foot-long Subway sandwich, and the third nudge was giving him ten dollars when he got to the Salvation Army. I wished him well and left. Do you know who received the greatest blessing? Wherever that man is today, I doubt that he remembers my acts of kindness, but twenty years later, I am still receiving blessings from that small act of giving.

The Bible teaches us how to give and provides us wonderful examples. One of the first examples in the New Testament is that of the magi, who came joyfully with the finest of gifts. "They had opened their treasures, they presented unto him gifts; gold, and frankincense and myrrh."[15] They came to worship the newborn King and present him with the best they had to offer. How does this contrast with the widow who dropped in two coins worth a penny into the offering plate? The story told in Mark teaches us much about giving. Jesus watched the crowds putting money into the temple treasury. Many of the rich people gave large amounts, and a poor widow managed only a few cents, but Jesus responded, "Truly I tell you, this poor widow has put more into the treasury then all the others. They all gave out of their wealth, but she out of her poverty, put in everything all she had."[16] The gift of the Magi and the gift of the widow were done out of love and in honor of God. They were done cheerfully.

How are we to give?

> Each of you should give what you have decided in your heart to give, not reluctantly or under compulsion, for God loves a cheerful giver.[17]

> Freely ye have received, freely give.[18]

> Give generously to him and do so without a grudging heart; then because of this the Lord your God will bless you in all your work and everything you put your hands on.[19]

Charge them that are rich in this world, that they be not high minded, nor trust in uncertain riches, but in the living God, who giveth us richly all things to enjoy. That they do good, that they be rich in good works, ready to distribute, willing to communicate; laying up in store for themselves a good foundation against the time to come, that they may hold on eternal life.[20]

These verses teach much about how to give. First, giving is a choice. We learned to understand that giving pleases God, and once we have made the choice, we are to give generously yet responsibly. We are to give from the heart all that we are able, understanding that giving is a privilege. The willingness to give cheerfully is more important than the amount. Understand that giving is an act of worship. There is an integrity to giving, and what counts is our honor in the sight of God and not humankind. The proper attitude toward giving is essential, as giving is ultimately about pleasing God.

At the same time, God expects us to use what has been given to us wisely. We all have financial commitments in life, so when you give, you must give wisely. Give in proportion to what God has given you. Give from what you have and not from what you don't have. Even when you give sacrificially, one must be responsible. We should always follow through on previous promises. Pledges made should be pledges kept.

We should also keep an open mind on how we can give and serve others. Avoid self-imposed limitations on your giving. If nature has made you a giver, your hands are born open and so is your heart; though there may be times when your hands are empty, your heart is always full, and you can give out of your heart warm things, kind things, sweet things. Money is not the only expression of giving. How about your time, or your knowledge, or just love and a smile? We can always give something. We know that Christ's self-giving is the standard basis for our giving. Maximilian Kolbe was a Catholic priest during World War II and found himself in the brutal work camp at Auschwitz. After several successful escape attempts by other inmates, the command of the camp decided to set an example by selecting ten prisoners for execution through the process of starvation. One of the young prisoners selected pleaded that he had a wife and children. The Catholic priest volunteered, "Take me, as I am willing to give my life for his." The ultimate sacrifice was made. At the end of two weeks, the last person still alive was the old Catholic priest. He raised up his arms in glory to God before being shot and thus ended a special testimony. Giving comes with so many opportunities of service and ways to honor God. Don't limit yourself when opportunities to give present themselves.

Though we should all experience the joy of giving, I believe some are given a special gift for giving. Those people use the assets of their time, money, and possessions wisely. They recognize their available resources and draw on them when needed. The giver can be prompted to give even when the need is not obvious. The giver has no real need for recognition as his or her reward is in the giving and not in the praise he or she might receive. The giver provides gifts that will last, as the quality of the gift is important to the giver. The giver will express gratitude toward God for allowing him or her to be able to give according to his or her abundance. Finally, a giver will encourage others to give so that others may experience the joy of giving. Giving indeed is a spiritual gift.

People do not give to reap rewards. However, that is exactly what happens when we give unselfishly from the heart and not expecting anything in return. This is a tried-and-true biblical principle that should be everyone's guide to successful living. A giving attitude is certainly one of the secrets to successful living. Examine these scriptures as they reveal the rewards one receives for generous, unselfish giving.

> Give and it will be given to you. A good measurable pressed down, shaken together and running over, will be poured onto your lap, for with the measure you use, it will be measured to you.[21]

> The generous man will be prosperous, whoever refreshes others will be refreshed.[22]

> The generous will themselves be blessed, for they share their food with the poor.[23]

> When you give to the needy, do not let your left hand
> know what your right hand is doing, so that your giving
> may be in secret. Then your Father who sees what is done
> in secret will reward you.[24]

> Every man according as he purposeth in his heart, so let
> him give; not grudgingly, or of necessity; for God loveth
> a cheerful giver.[25]

"It is in giving that we receive," said Francis of Assisi. I am by nature a typically stingy person, which is unfortunate, since my best memories involve giving. My prayer and your prayer every day should be, "Lord, help me be a more giving person." When I look at the great leaders of modern history, I find people who genuinely served others. The great automaker Henry Ford said, "The highest use of money is not to make more, but to make money to do more service for the betterment of life."

It is not a coincidence that the greatest givers seem to never run out of things to give. Bill Gates and Warren Buffett are two of the wealthiest men in the world. They are also two of the greatest givers in the world. I believe that the only thing that stops us from living an abundant life is our unwillingness to give from what we have been blessed. David McGee, author of *Cross the Bridge to Life,* said, "What we spend we lose, what we keep will be left for others, what we give away will be ours forever." The story of the businessman and philanthropist R. G. LeTourneau is one of interest that expresses this principle. He decided that instead of giving 10 percent and keeping 90 percent, he would do just the opposite. The result was that he became wealthier. His explanation was, "I shovel out the money, and God shovels it back, but God has a bigger shovel."

Though giving is truly a spiritual principle and "God so loved that he gave," the principle of giving leads to a more fulfilling life and a more rewarding and abundant one for anyone who experiences the joy of giving. The great American novelist Stephen King shared his personal story on giving, and it is paraphrased something like this: Involved in a car accident that left him facedown in a muddy creek, he realized that "when you're lying in a ditch with broken glass in your hair, no one accepts the Master Card in your back pocket," and that "we come into this life naked and broke, and we may be dressed when we go out, but we are still just as broke." Bill Gates, broke! Warren Buffett, broke! Stephen King, broke! All that you have is on loan, and all that remains is what you pass on. A life of giving, not just money but time and spirit, repays.

The great father of India, Gandhi, said, the best way to find yourself is to lose yourself in service to others. "If you want to touch the past touch a rock, if you want to touch the present touch a flower, but if you want to touch the future touch a life."

"For God so loved that he gave," and he gave so that we might have abundant and eternal life. If you are looking for a richer life, a more rewarding life, and a more abundant life, start by giving of yourself to others. Make a difference in your life and in our world today by loving and giving to others.

GRATITUDE

> This is the day which the Lord hath made:
> we will rejoice and be glad in it.
>
> —Psalm 118:24

"This is the day which the world has made; we will rejoice and be glad in it." My mother started every day with this Bible verse. Rain or shine, warm weather or cold, feeling good or in ill health, she was determined to make each day a special gift from God. That type of attitude is a winning attitude and one we should all strive to achieve.

What is attitude? According to Webster, it is the position or posture of the body in connection with an action, feeling, or mood. It is a manner of acting, feeling, or thinking that shows our disposition, opinion, or mindset. What is gratitude? It is a feeling of thankful appreciation for favors or benefits received. What is our disposition or temperament? It is the normal or prevailing aspect of one's nature, the balance of traits manifested in one's behavior or thinking.

How important is an attitude of gratitude? The answer is quite simple; it is the key to having a successful, productive, and joyful life. Understanding that life is precious and that it is a gift from God is the first step in making each day a great day. "Thanks be to God for his unspeakable gift."[1]

Legendary UCLA basketball coach John Wooden had a motto: "Make each day a masterpiece, and if you do that you will have a great week." Two things under your control are your effort and your attitude. If you think about it, the quality of your day depends on you. When you wake up in the morning, "consecrate yourselves today to the Lord … that He may bestow upon you a blessing this day."[2] When we wake up in the morning and give thanks to the Lord for the day he has made, when we realize the gift he has given us, and we dedicate ourselves to God and expect his blessings to be poured out on us, we have established an attitude of gratitude.

How do we make that type of attitude help us achieve our goals and the success we want in life? It all comes back to the gift of today. When you are prepared to make the most of every moment, you are ready to make the most of every day. As a teacher, I came to understand that the more prepared I was for a classroom setting, the better the learning experience for my students. I was always amazed at the calm disposition John Wooden displayed as a coach during games, but I came to understand that it was his preparation before the game that allowed his teams to succeed.

His teams were prepared to win. They made the most of every practice, and by making the most of every practice and being determined to be better every day, they accomplished historic records in college basketball. When you make the most of every day, tomorrow will automatically be better.

A key word in that statement is *make*. Making the most of every day means that you are in charge. You can have a positive attitude. You can set goals. You can take planned steps to achieve those goals. You can focus on achieving excellence, where good enough is never good enough. You can live each day to the fullest—one that is focused on joy, helping others, living wisely, living effectively, and investing your life in the people around you.

God has given us 86,400 seconds this day to use as we choose. How will you use them? What will your attitude be? Psalms gives us a clue as to what our attitude should be—one of thanks.

> O give thanks to the Lord for he is good, his steadfast love endures forever.[3]

> O give thanks unto the Lord for he is good, for his mercy endureth forever.[4]

> Bless the Lord, O my soul, and forget not all his benefits.[5]

Do not forget the benefits of today and how you can use them. I have always considered the Bible as the road map to successfully guide us on the road of life. God's Word provides us examples of how to live life abundantly and how to avoid failures and disasters in life. One character that has always intrigued me was Jacob's son, Joseph. His attitude through life allowed him to navigate the many pitfalls he faced and to do it successfully.

Four thousand years ago, a seventeen-year-old boy learned what an arrogant attitude can lead to. In Joseph's case, it led to the bottom of a well and ultimately being sold for twenty shekels of silver by ten brothers that Joseph had totally alienated. I can only imagine what Joseph must have thought as he lay alone in the bottom of that well or as he trudged along in chains through the desert on the road to slavery in Egypt. It was during this time, though, that you see Joseph's attitude change to one of humility and of allowing God to work in his life.

Potiphar, an officer of Pharaoh and captain of the guard, bought Joseph. The Lord was with Joseph, and Potiphar was able to see this. Potiphar trusted Joseph and placed him in charge of his complete household. It turned out to be a wise decision, as Joseph and Potiphar's house prospered. Joseph had the proper attitude. He would make each day an excellent day. He focused on the task at hand and served his master well. By using the hours of each day to achieve excellence, both he and his master prospered.

A second attitude was seen at Potiphar's house, an attitude to remain true to his convictions and not to waiver when confronted with temptation. The story goes that Potiphar's wife had designs to sleep with Joseph, but Joseph refused, displaying an attitude of loyalty to his master and steadfast faith to his morals and to his God. "How then can I do this great wickedness, and sin against God?"[6]

Yet again, Joseph found turmoil in his life as Potiphar's wife convinced her husband that Joseph was guilty, and Joseph found himself in prison. It would be easy to give up at this juncture, but Joseph had a conquering attitude. With God's help, he would not be defeated. Joseph found favor in the sight of the keeper of the prison and before long was left in charge of the other prisoners. "Whatsoever they did there, he was the doer of it."[7] Joseph must have had an attitude of making every minute count for something good. Nothing should be taken for granted. "When times are good, be happy, but when times are bad consider this: God has made the one as well as the other."[8]

While Joseph was in prison, he met the butler and baker to Pharaoh's court, and we see another attitude that served Joseph well; he noticed their sad countenances and cared enough to listen to them. Our attitude each day should include investing our lives in the people around us. Joseph's investment in the life of Pharaoh's butler turned out to be his ticket out of prison. The butler remembered Joseph, and Pharaoh called for Joseph to interpret his troublesome dreams. The ultimate interpretation of the dream was this: Egypt would have seven years of plenty followed by seven years of famine.

Joseph's attitude in front of Pharaoh is one of confident humility. The Lord had brought him through many tragic situations to prepare him for this time and place. "The answer is not in me; God shall give pharaoh an answer of peace."[9]

That attitude of confident humility is seen by Joseph's next suggestion, to find a man discreet and wise and set him over the land of Egypt to handle the monumental task this nation would face. Pharaoh's answer was, "For as much as God hath showed thee all of this, there is none so discrete and wise as thou art."[10] Wow, in thirteen years Joseph had gone from the bottom of the well to ruler over all the land of Egypt. How did he do it? He realized that each day is a gift from God, that no matter the circumstances we should make every minute count, and that time spent in preparation for those special moments will pay off.

Joseph also had an attitude of preparation. If Egypt were to successfully weather the storms of the next fourteen years, it must prepare properly. Joseph knew success could only be achieved through hard work and careful planning. One of the great advertising slogans of today is Nike's "Just Do It" slogan. Successful people do it; they have an attitude of accomplishment, to work each day as if it were their last. Procrastination is unacceptable. Joseph trusted the Lord and knew from experience that with God all things are possible.

How about the rest of the story? The famine of seven years affected not only Egypt, but all the land that surrounded Egypt. That famine brought a starving family of brothers who had betrayed Joseph and sold him to Egypt. We see another side of Joseph—an attitude of compassion, love, and forgiveness. Joseph took them in and made them comfortable. Two verses indicate Joseph's attitude of forgiveness.

Be not grieved nor angry with yourselves, that ye sold me hither: for God did send me before you to preserve life.[11]

But as for you; ye thought evil against me, but God meant it unto good.[12]

Even the names of Joseph's children reveal much about his attitude and who should get the glory. Manasseh, his firstborn, means, "God made me forget my hardships." His second son was named Ephraim, meaning, "God has prospered me."

After a long, full life, Joseph died at 110 years of age. What can we glean from Joseph's character? Here was a man favored by God because of his humility, his nobility, his morality, his fidelity, his patience, his perseverance, his iron will, and his positive attitude that "this is the day the Lord has made and I will rejoice and be glad in it."

A positive attitude is not the only thing necessary in life, but it may well be the most important thing. I am reminded of a story of two families who moved into our town recently and asked what kind of people lived here. The wise man simply asked them what kind of people lived in the town where they had lived before. They answered, "Great people, warm and caring."

"You are in luck" said the old man, "you will find the same kind of people here."

The second family asked the same question, to which the old man responded in the same way. The second family answered, "They were cold and unfriendly," to which the old man replied, "Sorry, folks, but I am afraid you will find this town to be the same." Look for the best in every place, and believe the best about every person, and that is probably what you will find.

What would happen if we all saw each other as important? Everyone is here for a purpose, and everyone has great possibilities. We need to keep a positive attitude about every person we meet because that person may make all the difference in your life. Remember the butler that impacted Joseph's life. People like Joseph look for the positive in everything because they realize the gift of each day. Joseph bloomed where he was planted.

Your attitude more than anything else will determine whether you are a success or a failure, happy or miserable.

Joseph is a wonderful example of a great attitude, but he is not the perfect example. We look to Jesus Christ as the perfect example.

> Who is the image of the invisible God, the first born of every creature.[13]

> As the Spirit of the Lord works within us, we are being transformed into His image with ever increasing Glory.[14]

Throughout the New Testament, we are told to make every effort to become like Jesus. "Put on the new self, created to be like God in true righteousness and holiness."[15] We are told to do all things in a Christlike manner. God does not want us to become God, but he does want us to become godly.

How do we best describe the attitude of Christ? By looking at the cross much is revealed about his attitude. In the seven phrases recorded in the Gospel we see much about his character: forgiveness—"Father forgive them, for they not know what they do."[16] Compassion, as he looked on one of the thieves and said, "Verily I say unto you, today shalt thou be with me in paradise."[17] Obedience, determination, and sacrifice in carrying out God's plan—"It is finished."[18] Finally confidence—"Into thy hands I commend my spirit."[19]

Not only does the cross reveal much about his attitude; his ministry allows us to see so much more. His three-year ministry represents time well spent—days not wasted. We must first consider an attitude of humility and an attitude of servanthood. Your attitude should be the same as that of Christ Jesus, "who being in very nature God, did not consider equality with God something to be used to his own advantage, rather he made himself nothing, by taking the very nature of a servant, being made in human likeness."[20]

We see also his compassion, kindness, and willingness to give himself to others. His healing of the blind, the lame, the lepers, and the mute shows us his empathy for our physical needs. His willingness to accept everyone and listen to the needs of everyone shows us an attitude of equality for all. His meeting with the woman at the well and the wisdom and care he showed for the woman about to be stoned for adultery reveal an attitude of universal acceptance and love for all. His Sermon on the Mount reveals his wisdom and his communication skills. He was forceful yet gentle, authoritative yet understanding. The greatest part of his attitude was that of unconditional love. "For God so loved the world, that he gave his only son, that whosoever believeth in him should not perish, but have everlasting life."[21] Jesus lived every day knowing that his mission was to die on the cross as the ultimate sacrifice for our sins. Yet every day, I believe he arose with an attitude of this is the day the Lord has made.

The love of God and the sacrifice Jesus made should make each day a special day for us. The life he has given us is an exciting one, so don't miss it. Even when the road of life gets rough, we can learn from it, and those tough times can have a positive influence on us. Don't let problems of the past and anxiety about tomorrow cause you to miss the blessings of today.

Godliness with contentment is great gain.[22]

Giving thanks always, for all things to God and the Father in the name of our Lord Jesus Christ.[23]

Do you need an attitude adjustment? We have all been given the priceless gift of another day to live. As Christians we should be filled with genuine thanksgiving. We should be filled with an enthusiasm that produces positive results. Remember every day presents new opportunities to serve God and others, and in the process of doing good works we can find great joy and be able to genuinely say, "This is the day which the Lord hath made, we will rejoice and be glad in it."

HOPE

For I know the plans I have for you, declares the Lord, plans to prosper
you and not to harm you, plans to give you hope and a future.
—Jeremiah 29:11 (NIV)

Does God have a plan for your life? The book of truths, the Word of God,
gives us an undeniable answer—absolutely. Just as God had a plan for
Jeremiah, he has a plan for you. He not only has a plan for your life; he
has a plan for your day, and that plan is not to harm you but to prosper
you, to give you a hope, and a future.

Who was the prophet of God that gives us such a powerful and positive
message from the Lord? Jeremiah lived and prophesied during troubled
times that ultimately led to the fall of Jerusalem in 587 BC. Like a voice
in the wilderness, this man of God prayed, preached, suffered, wrote, and
above all believed. His message was simple: a disobedient people needed
to change their moral course, or disaster would follow. Jeremiah lived
in disruptive times, and so do we, yet because of God's grace and love,
Jeremiah gives us a message of hope in this powerful verse. It helps us
understand why we are here, what our purpose is, what God's plan for us is,
and that we will prosper and experience the good life by following his plan.

On September 28, 1949, I was born, and biblical truths tell me that
God already had a plan for me. "Before I formed thee in the belly I knew
thee, and before thou comest forth out of the womb I sanctified thee."[1] I
believe this to be true for all of God's children. However, given our free
will and our nature to pursue our own destiny, we as humans often choose
a different path.

My first decision was to choose obedience and follow God's plan, and
at seventeen I felt called to the ministry. My seventeenth summer was a

happy one as I followed the will of the Lord and the plan that he had for me and became a young preacher. College came in the fall, and a new world opened to me. New choices presented themselves, and I made the decision that I knew what was best for me, and God's plan would have to wait.

The next decade I lived a very secular life. Marriage, good times, and a good job seemed to suggest that I was on the right track. Yet an emptiness within my soul suggested otherwise. The reason to me was obvious; I was not following God's plan.

After careful consideration and prayer, I put out a fleece and asked God to dramatically reveal his plan for my life. The fleece was this: that pastor Bill Dudley, who was my minister at seventeen, would contact me. I had not heard from Bill in ten years, but that night he called. We discussed what God was doing in my life, and a special truth of the Bible became abundantly clear: "the Lord, He it is that doth go before thee, He will be with thee, He will not fail thee, neither forsake thee."[2] Though I had drifted away from his will, the Lord was still by my side. God leads you in the direction you need to take.

At this point I made the worst decision of my life. I chose disobedience, I chose my pride, and I chose what I deemed best for me. Big mistake; God's way is always better than humankind's way. The next couple of years became a disaster highlighted by a failed marriage and many days searching how I could make my world right again. If only I had walked hand in hand with God, this low point in my life could have been avoided.

It would be another ten years before I felt God's call upon my life. This time I listened and obeyed, but God's plans for me had changed. No longer could he use me as a minister, but through life's experiences he had adequately prepared me as a teacher and coach. First as a Sunday school teacher, the Lord matured me as a Christian to the point where I could touch the lives of young people. For the last ten years in the classroom of a Christian school and on the sports fields of middle schools and high schools I have tried to serve the Lord. The result is the joy promised in Jeremiah to prosper you, to give you hope and a future. Does God have a plan for you? He absolutely does. Make no mistake, God has a plan for everyone. The questions to ask are these: Are you doing God's work? Are you at the center of his will? Is he leading you, and are you following?

"For I know." Know is defined as having a clear perception or understanding of, to be sure or well informed about. In biblical terms, it also means to approve or take delight. As our heavenly Father, God delights in his children and our discoveries, and the all-knowing God has planned something good for us. In the Sermon on the Mount, Jesus Christ teaches us not to worry; your heavenly Father knows your needs. Worry is like a rocking chair; it gives you something to do, but it doesn't get you anywhere. Many years ago there was a television show called *Father Knows Best*. Your first step to having a life of purpose, a life of fulfillment and joy, is to understand that our heavenly Father knows what is best for his children. When we obediently follow the Father's will, we begin to live a life of abundance.

The Lord has plans for you—Our God is a God who plans. Think of the boundless glories of our universe and the infinite planning necessary to create a planet that can sustain life. The balance that exists in our universe is almost unimaginable, yet *impossible* is one of God's favorite words. Think of it this way; if you accomplish a possible dream, you get the glory. If you accomplish an impossible dream, God gets the glory.

The human body is a miracle. Think of the millions of things inside of our bodies that must work for us to function as we do. A simple cell has more parts that must work together in an organized fashion than the average person can comprehend. Think of the planning to create and sustain such a world.

Does God have a plan for you?

"Plans to give you hope." Hope is defined as desire accompanied by expectation. It is a feeling that what is wanted will happen. Our God is a God of hope. The psalms are full of hope.

My hope comes from Him.[3]

Thou art my hope, o Lord God, Thou art my trust from my youth.[4]

Put your hope in the Lord, both now and forever.[5]

Anyone who is among the living has hope.[6]

Now the God of Hope fill you with all joy, and peace in believing that ye may abound in hope through the power of the Holy ghost.[7]

Our God is a God with plans for you—plans to prosper you and give you hope.

"Plans to give … a future"—Future is defined as something about to be, what is to come, what will happen. Our heavenly Father has plans for your future, and it is a bright one. It starts with a reverence for God.

Be thou in the fear of the Lord all the day long.[8]

So shall the knowledge of wisdom be unto thy soul: when thou has found it, then there shall be a reward, and thy expectations shall not be cut off.[9]

How do we figure out these plans that will give us fulfillment, bring us joy, prosper us, and give us hope for the future? Constantly ask questions and wait for answers. Pray, read the Bible, share your life with others, seek their advice and God's advice, and expect an answer. When the answer comes, follow his plan.

You know, God created us in his image. He gave us a brain designed for great things. What you want to be, where you want to go, what you love to do, projects you hope to achieve, goals you want to reach, all those things are God-inspired. God gives us great ideas, and he expects in return human achievements worthy of glorifying God. God is glorified by the great victories of his people. "For we are his workmanship, created in Christ Jesus unto good works which God hath before ordained that we should walk in them."[10]

Are my dreams too big for God's plan? Can I really be used in a mighty way? Those men that changed the world were cleaning fish before they heeded the call: "Follow Me." Abraham was a liar; Moses was a murderer; David was an adulterer; Matthew was a tax collector; Gomer and Rahab were prostitutes. Failures and setbacks can be positive possibilities.

Our past experiences define what God may have before us. Simple questions may provide answers to what God's plan is. Where has he led us before? What am I most passionate about? We all have been given gifts—something uniquely suited to you—and often we know what that gift is.

I am reminded of a great prayer: Open my eyes to see the incredible opportunities that are before me today and give me enough common sense never to slam a door shut that you have just opened.

As I dig into that scripture, I am again reminded of Ephesians 2:10. We are created for good works. God planned that we should spend our lives helping others. We were put on earth to contribute, to make a difference with our lives, and when we do, we will find fulfillment. The satisfaction and joy that one feels is part of the prosperity, hope, and future Jeremiah talks about.

"Be strong in the Lord and in the power of his might."[11] When you believe that with God's help there is a lot more within you than you have ever experienced, you can discover the power that allows you to pursue your objectives, accomplish your goals, and abide in God's plan for your life. Open your mind and let the thoughts of God and his positive plans change your life to be prosperous—one of hope and a future.

When you are obedient and follow God's plans, you carry an attitude of anticipation. What is next? "Tomorrow the Lord will do wonders among you."[12] What a powerful statement. We need to believe that tomorrow will be even better than today. The late John Wooden lived by the decree "make each day a masterpiece." When we let God plan our day and by faith trust in tomorrow, we can keep our eyes fixed firmly on the goal. We can seize every new opportunity with confidence.

Colossians 4:17 speaks well to the work the Lord has set before you. "Take heed to the ministry to which you have received in the Lord, that thou may fulfill it."[13] I am reminded of the retired college professor who took work at a convenience store in order to meet people and have a positive impact in service to others. Trust in God's plan and understand a good work is waiting for you today.

When does God's plan for our life end? That is simple—when we do. Look back at the life of Christ. As a young boy he went to the temple and amazed the temple priests as he went about his Father's business. As a young man he prepared himself for God's plan, and his three-year ministry changed the world. Remember his last words from the cross: "It is finished." By following God's plan, Christ has offered us eternal life, prosperity, and hope for the future.

God has a plan for us no matter what our age may be. Are you looking ahead with hope or back with disappointment? I choose to live and succeed by continuing to look forward with hope. A good friend once told me that Satan created retirement age at sixty-five. We are called to service, and though that service may change, God does not want us to retire. I am reminded of the woman who lost her husband at the age of sixty-three and was convinced that the end of her life would soon follow and waited another twenty-four years for that to come. When you live to be one hundred, you will look back and realize how young you were when you were sixty-five.

My dear mother died when she was eighty-three, and the last year of her life was a struggle. In those difficult times, she often asked the question, "Why am I still here?" Yet God had a plan for her life, and that plan was not finished. A seventeen-year-old grandson trying to find his way needed her words of wisdom. On the Sunday afternoon before she died on Tuesday, the two of them had a talk that would lead to a spiritual awakening for my son. He would later say that his view of life changed after visiting his grandmother for the last time. The next day she had completed her mission, and she lapsed into a coma and passed away. Her hope for the future was now one of eternal life.

Are you looking ahead with hope or back with disappointment? I choose to look forward with hope. I can do that through the faith that God has a plan for my life, a plan to bring me fulfillment, joy, and prosperity— plans to give me hope and a future.

FAITH

Truly I tell you, if you have faith as small as a mustard seed,
you can say to this mountain, move from here to there and
it will move. Nothing will be impossible for you.
—Matthew 17:20–21 (NIV)

Believe it, and you can achieve it. That simple statement is used over and over by athletic coaches in every sport at every level. The reason is simple: it is true. When we talk about believing, when we talk about faith, it is important to understand that the more you believe and the more faith you have in something or someone, the more positive will be the outcome.

The experiences I have had in coaching sports have taught me that my greatest success stories revolve around teams that believed they would be successful and teams that had faith in one another. In the summer of 2007, I had the pleasure of coaching a fifth-grade girls' basketball team. The collection of girls that I had were driven to be the best, and they believed they would win every game. After winning several tournaments, we set our sights on the Mid American Youth Basketball (MAYB) National Tournament. We played well, and after winning our first five games, found ourselves in the finals against a team called Kansas City Elite. The name itself suggests just how good this team was. At halftime we were down 31–10, and I began to tell my girls what a great season we had played, and there was nothing wrong in finishing second in a national tournament, especially to a team that was bigger, quicker, and more skilled than our little group from Newkirk and Ponca City, Oklahoma. That is when a group of ten-year-old girls taught me a valuable lesson. First one girl and then another said they believed we could win, and by the end of the half, I had a completely reenergized team and a coach that was feeling that all things are possible. The girls played their hearts out, and by the end of the third quarter we were down by twelve, and I was starting to believe. Hope continued to build during the fourth quarter, and with less than a minute to play, we found ourselves down by three, and we had the ball. Great effort and an offensive rebound cut the lead to one with less than thirty seconds to play, and a miracle was within our grasp. Then it happened; an Elite player hit a shot, and we missed ours. The final score was 43–40.

However, an extremely valuable lesson was learned by eight little girls and their coach. When you believe in something, when you have faith that you can accomplish something, then all things become possible. We walked off the court that day with our heads held high knowing that we did not quit and understanding that when you really believe in something, all things are possible.

The value of belief, the value of faith in real life, cannot be understated, and the purpose of this chapter is to show you that through faith, through a steadfast belief system, you can move mountains.

The Bible gives us the perfect definition of faith in Hebrews 11:1. "Faith is the substance of things hoped for, the evidence of things not seen." It is a belief, a trust, especially in a higher power. It is a firm belief in something for which there appears to be no scientific proof. It is a trust, assurance, and confidence in God, and our faith is shown by our service and obedience to God. Faith comes before a prayer is answered and before an individual has received what he or she has requested from God. Faith is believing that God watches over us, cares for us, and hears our prayers. Faith is believing that God not only hears our prayers but will answer our prayers, even in ways we cannot imagine. Faith is the belief that God will always do the right thing, not necessarily what we want at the time, but always the right thing. There is a quiet certainty about faith. One's faith is sure and certain. The beginning point of that faith is believing in God's promises that he will do what he says he will do. When we believe that God will fulfill his promises even though we don't see those promises materialize yet, we demonstrate true faith.

The greatest example of faith found in the Old Testament is Father Abraham. The Lord tells Abraham to "get thee out of thy country, and from thy kindred, and from thy father's house, unto a land that I will shew you, and I will make of thee a great nation, and I will bless thee, and make thy name great."[1] We see Abraham's response: "So Abraham departed ... and Lot went with him, and Abraham was seventy and five years when he departed."[2]

Abraham's faith begins with a journey. Abraham believed that God's words were true and that he would perform all that he promised. He believed that nothing was too hard for God. He trusted and believed that God would guide him. Faith is a walk; it is a journey, and people like Abraham who walk in faith are never ultimately defeated.

Abraham sojourned in a strange country because he had faith that God would guide his steps. Sara, at the age of ninety, conceived a son, because she judged God faithful who had promised. It was by faith that Abraham was willing to offer up Isaac on the alter, "accounting that God was able to raise him up, even from the dead."[3] With God all things are possible.

Today, Abraham has earned a special place in world history—from God's promises that he would be the father of many nations, that he would be successful in the world, and that he would become a father at one hundred years old. It is important to understand the role of faith in that reality. By trusting his guidance and direction, by trusting in God's promises, by demonstrating his faith through obedience, Abraham achieved what God had promised. Three of the great religions of the modern era (Judaism, Christianity, and Islam) all trace their lineage to Father Abraham. Because of his faith, Abraham was justified before God, and his faith was accounted to him for righteousness.

A second example of great faith found in the Old Testament is the story of Shadrach, Meshach, and Abednego who refused to bow down to King Nebuchadnezzar or to worship false Gods and faced death because of it. Daniel 3:17–18 reveals their unyielding faith. "If it be so, our God whom we serve is able to deliver us from the burning fiery furnace, and he will deliver us out of thy hand, O King. But if not, be it known unto thee, O King, that we will not serve thy Gods, nor worship the golden image thou hast set up."[4] We know the rest of the story; the three were thrown into the fiery furnace, but the fire had no power over them, and they became a testimony to all of Babylon and especially the king. Their faith was the substance of what they hoped for, and it was the evidence of that which had not been received. They believe they would be delivered because they obeyed God, but they also believed that God would do what was right.

At the core of my beliefs, at the very heart of my faith, is the fact that belief and faith bring positive results. The story of the two blind men that come to Jesus in Matthew 9:27–30 is a simple account that yields a powerful statement on faith. Two blind men came to Jesus asking to be healed, and Jesus asked one simple question: "Believe ye that I am able to do this?" Their answer was simple: "Yes, Lord." Then he touched their eyes, saying, "according to your faith be it unto you."[5] Their eyes were opened, and they could see.

Countless scriptures speak to the power of faith and the positive outcome of believing in God's promises.

> All things in faith, whatsoever ye shall ask in prayer, believing, ye shall receive.[6]

> Have faith in God. What things soever ye desire, when ye pray, believe that ye receive them, and ye shall have them.[7]

> For with God, nothing shall be impossible.[8]

Of course, the power of faith and the positive outcome of faith is based on the promises and character of God.

> Faithful is he that calleth you, who also will do it.[9]

> The Lord is faithful, he shall establish you, and keep you from evil.[10]

> Let us hold fast the profession of our faith without wavering, for he is faithful that promised.[11]

It is important to understand that our faithfulness is based on the faithfulness of God.

What is the value of positive faith? With positive faith we expect positive results. We have an inner sense that things are going to work out all right, that better days are ahead, that storms will pass, that mountains have peaks, and that darkness gives way to light. It was with positive faith that Joshua marched around Jericho seven times, and the walls came tumbling down. It is positive faith that gives us enthusiasm and a second wind as we face life's challenges and allows us to come back after being defeated. "Let us not grow weary while doing good, for in due season we shall reap a harvest, if we do not lose heart."[12] God will provide faith when you need it the most. Think of it this way, if God inspired you to begin, he will surely guide you to succeed. "He which hath begun a good work in you will perform it until the day of Christ Jesus."[13] The power of faith helps us endure to the end and in fact can help us remain alive, active, and enthusiastic until the end of our journey.

Exercising our faith puts our faith into action; it becomes a positive force that allows us to believe it and achieve it. It allows us to stretch our limits and boundaries and believe that with God all things are indeed possible. The more we stretch our limitations, the farther we get, and the mountains we confront are moved or become simple hills to climb over. Impossible situations become possible miracles. Understand that the Lord empowers those who know him and faithfully serve him. It is said of champions that they believe they will experience winning. They believe their best days are in front of them. If you want to be a champion, grow your faith. By doing so you will understand the purpose of life—to fulfill the plan God has for your life.

So how do we grow our faith? First, ask God for more faith.

> If any of you lack wisdom, you should ask God, who gives generously … but you must believe and not doubt.[14]

> He that cometh to God must believe that he is, and that he is a rewarder of them that diligently seek Him.[15]

> Ask and it shall be given you, seek and ye shall find, knock and it shall be opened unto you.[16]

> This is the confidence that we have in him, that if we ask anything according to his will, he heareth us.[17]

Second, focus on obeying God. God expects our faith to produce good works. There is no such thing as having faith without works, and when we obey God, our faith grows. "Suppose a brother or sister is without clothes and daily food. If one of you says to them "Go in peace, keep warm, and well fed; but does nothing about their physical needs, what good is it? In the same way, faith by itself, if it is not accompanied by action, is dead."[18]

Third, put God's Word in your mind. "Faith comes by hearing, and hearing by the word of God."[19] The Bible is the place to find God's promises, and those promises are too many to enumerate in this chapter. But a glimpse of such promises include: that he will provide our spiritual and physical needs, that he will never leave us or forsake us, that he will give us wisdom when we ask, that he will never allow our trials to be more than we can bear, that he will give us peace of mind, and that he will cause everything in our lives to eventually work out for good. This is God speaking to us through his Word.

The skeptic may ask for proof; the person of faith believes the proof is already there. The noted writer C. S. Lewis said, "I believe in Christianity as I believe the sun has risen, not only because I see it, but because by it, I see everything else." Ralph Waldo Emerson gives us these words of wisdom, "All I have seen teaches me to trust the Creator for all I have not seen." Corrie Ten Boom, during her trials in a Nazi concentration camp, gives us these positive words in faith and trust: "Never be afraid to trust an unknown future to a known God."

Why is our having faith important to God? Hebrews 11:6 tells us that without faith, it is impossible to please God. When we don't put our trust in God, we dishonor him. We essentially say that you are not who you say you are. We show our faith by our obedience and our service to him. Our faith is perfected as we do his will. Jesus Christ offers up the perfect prayer of faith: "O my father, if it be possible, let this cup pass from me, never the less not as I will, but as thou wilt."[20] When we believe that God knows best, we are free to ask anything from God, and if it is part of God's wise and perfect will for our lives it will be granted.

We all face seemingly impossible spiritual mountains. They can be moved through faith and God's promises that he will increase our faith if we fervently ask and draw close to him. How I wish our nation's leaders had this type of faith. George Washington, our nation's first president, kept a prayer diary, and I recently read an excerpt that helps explain why he was able to believe in the impossible. "Purge my heart by the Holy Spirit that I may of more freedom of mind and liberty of will serve thee, the everlasting

God, in righteousness and holiness this day, and all the days of my life. Increase the faith ... pardon my wandering and direct thoughts unto you." How powerful, how positive. What a quality of leadership is expressed in these words. Did God honor and bless our first president for his faith? The answer is a resounding yes.

I wish to strive for an effective faith, one that depends on God and willingness to do his will, a faith that becomes stronger in the presence of life's difficulties. I wish to have faith of hopeful anticipation that the best is yet to come. "Be thou faithful unto death, and I will give you a crown of life."[21] In the end, let it be said that I kept the faith and because of that faith I was either able to move my mountains, climb over them, or tunnel through them and win the final victory.

GUIDANCE

Thy word is a lamp unto my feet and a light unto my path.
—Psalm 119:105

As I sit in my office working on this chapter, I seek guidance. Not only do I seek guidance and direction on where this chapter should go, but I seek guidance and direction on where my life should go. For you see, this morning I received a call asking me to return to full-time teaching. At sixty-five, I thought it was time to retire, step out of the classroom, dabble in coaching, spend more time at home, travel and see the world, and quietly ride off into the sunset. How do I determine the right move? How do I determine the direction God would have me take? What is the way to find clarity in seeking godly guidance?

Why read the Bible? I believe godly guidance starts with God's Holy Word. The psalmist indicates that the holy scriptures are there to enlighten us and to guide us in life's journey. The Bible is God's road map on how to live a productive life. It reveals the nature and will of God, but it also shows us how to follow the right path and avoid the wrong one. The lamp that guides us is fed by the oil of the Holy Spirit. "When He the spirit of truth is come, he will guide you into all truth."[1]

The Bible is an inexhaustible source of knowledge and wisdom about life and the world around us. It presents us with friends, mentors, counselors, advisers, and encouragers. "Understand what thou readest? How can I, except some man should guide me."[2] We should be thirsty for the knowledge and wisdom we find in the Bible, for it is a living active counselor in your time of need.

The Bible has stood the test of time. Think about it! It was written over a period of sixteen centuries by forty different authors. Those authors included shepherds, soldiers, scholars, and fishermen. It was written in three different languages. Some of it was written in Arabia and some on the Mediterranean island of Patmos. Yet there is one singular theme—a loving God seeking to save his children. Three hundred prophecies about Christ were fulfilled five hundred years before his coming. The Bible works because it is the Word of God. For us to find godly guidance we must be familiar with his Word and trust in his Word. Could it be that it had one mind, one designer, one divine imprint? It has been a best seller since Gutenberg invented the printing press, and though governments have made it illegal and dictators burned it, it still thrives, and his Word continues.

His Word promises godly guidance. The very character of God is to direct us. He does this because he loves us and wants the best for us. Listen to these promises from God:

> I will bring the blind by a way that they knew not. I will lead them in paths they have not known: I will make darkness light before them, and crooked things straight. These will I do unto them and not forsake them.[3]

> He that hath mercy on them shall lead them, even by the springs of water shall He guide them.[4]

> The Lord shall guide thee continually, and satisfy thy soul in drought, and make fat thy bones: and thou shalt be like a watered garden, and like a spring of water, whose waters fail not.[5]

As we trust God and lean on the promises found in the Bible, he will lead us and direct our paths, especially when we asked for direction.

> Thou art my rock and my fortress; therefore, for thy name's sake, lead me and guide me.[6]

> Lead me O Lord in thy righteousness.[7]

Lead me in thy truth, and teach me; for thou art the God of my salvation.[8]

From the end of the earth will I cry unto thee, when my heart is overwhelmed: lead me to the rock that is higher than I.[9]

Teach me to do thy will; for thou art my God: thy spirit is good; lead me into the land of uprightness.[10]

In praying for godly guidance, it becomes abundantly clear that we must have an attitude of not my will, but thy will be done. Be familiar with his Word and live in subjection to his spirit. This will help us understand God's guidance in our lives. We must pray and maintain constant fellowship with God to recognize the paths God wants us to take. By prayerfully asking God to guide your life, you will be presented with amazing possibilities. Nothing quite generates self-confidence as powerfully as the conviction that you are being guided by God. Furthermore, godly guidance in our lives begins long before we are aware of what is happening.

I think back on the life of Moses. The Jewish people saw him as the deliverer, leader, lawgiver, great prophet, and governor of a nation. God directed his path for almost eighty years before he was even aware of that direction. His life is easily divided into three equal portions: life in Egypt, exile in Arabia, and deliverer of a nation.

Born around 1520 BC, it had been a pharaoh's dream about the birth of a Hebrew deliverer that allowed Moses to be placed in that tiny basket on the Nile River and discovered by Pharaoh's daughter. Adopted and considered Egyptian, he rose to prominence in the Egyptian hierarchy. He learned Egyptian ways and understood the strengths and weaknesses of the Egyptian royalty.

Upon discovering his true identity and through the slaying of an Egyptian overseer, Moses fled and was led to Midian, where he married Zipporah and became a sheepherder for his father-in-law, Jethro. It was there Moses received his call from God, a specific sign when an angel of the Lord appeared to Moses in a burning bush that would not be consumed. Two revelations were made to Moses that day: the external self-existence of one God and his mission to deliver his people. His first reaction was, "Not me, Lord. I am a man of few words." Yet God promised to lead, guide, and assist. Aaron, his brother, would be his spokesman. As you look at the life of Moses, you understand that God had led and directed Moses for eighty years for such a time as this.

As said before, when you know that you are being led by God, you can certainly gain a lot of self-confidence. I can't help but remember the scenes in the great movie *The Ten Commandments* when Moses approached Pharaoh. He did so with boldness and confidence. With each plague cast upon the nation of Egypt, Moses grew bolder and more confident that the nation of Israel would shake off the bondage of Egyptian slavery.

Divine direction led them to the Red Sea and a seemingly closed door opened wide as the nation of Israel crossed over on dry land, only to see the Egyptian army swallowed up by the sea. Moses continued to follow God's lead into the wilderness, and the miracles that followed are well documented in Exodus chapters 15–17. The bitter waters of Marah were sweetened. They were led to Elim where they found twelve wells of water and seventy palm trees. They were led into the wilderness where they were fed manna from heaven. They were led by a cloud in the day and a pillar of fire at night. They were led to Rephidian where the rock gave forth water. They were led to Sinai where Moses received the Ten Commandments. The point is they were lead, step-by-step. Moses, by accepting God's will and following his plan, became one of the most revered people in Hebrew history.

Moses knew who went before him and guided his path. "And the Lord, He it is that doth go before thee, He will be with thee, He will not fail thee, neither forsake thee, do fear not or be dismayed."[11] You should have no fear of the future if you are doing God's work that he has planned for you. You should face the future boldly if you are in the center of his will. He is leading, he is guiding, and you are following. You have this godly promise, "I will make all my mountains a way, and my highway shall be exalted."[12] Remember though, it is his road and his highway.

We have talked about godly guidance, but what is implied by someone who guides? Webster would define such a person as one who will show the way and lead, one who is thoroughly familiar with the course and connotes a continual presence of direction along the way. Several years ago, my wife and I took a guided tour in Alaska called "Bears and Eagles." As we walked through the wilderness for over an hour, our experienced guide pointed out the many wonders of the Alaskan wilderness, yet we still had not seen any bears or eagles, but I was enjoying the tour because of the knowledge of our guide. Then we came to a clearing where an Alaskan river teaming with salmon revealed one of the more breathtaking sights I have experienced—eagles and bears feasting on salmon. The guide who had led us through the wilderness had delivered and exceeded our expectations.

Another important way to receive godly guidance is through the counsel of Christians. A number of scriptures point us in this direction.

> Where no counsel is, the people fall; but in the multitude
> of counselors there is safety.[13]

> The integrity of the upright shall guide them.[14]

In seeking out godly guidance, go to his holy Word, pray for his leadership, and turn to people of integrity—people you trust to provide godly advice. Oftentimes by seeking God's guidance, he will direct you to just the person who needs to touch your life and give you the sense of peace that when you come to that fork in the road and the choice is made, you know you have chosen the right path.

Guidance also comes through our best reasonable thinking and that inner voice of our feelings. "I will praise the Lord, who counsels me, even at night my heart instructs me."[15] When we exercise trust and acknowledge God in all things, he will guide us. We do not even have to be aware that he is guiding us. When our motives and goals are right, guidance will happen. Most of God's guidance is part of our unconscious. "Trust in the Lord with all your heart and lean not unto thine own understanding, in all thy ways acknowledge him and he shall direct thy paths."[16]

God wants us to use the brain he gave us. He even tells us quite bluntly what he expects. "I will instruct you and teach thee in the way which thou shalt go, I will guide thee with mine eye. Don't be like the horse or the mule, which have no understanding, whose mouth must be held in with *bit* and bridle."[17] If God gives us wisdom to know what is the best path to take, that is just as much his guidance as giving some miraculous sign.

Reading the Bible, praying for guidance, seeking advice from Christian mentors, and grappling with the decisions are all part of the maturity process. They are all part of the faith process. Oswald Chambers, an early twentieth century evangelist, said, "Faith never knows where it is being led, but it loves and knows the one who is leading."

Remember, God cares about the details of your life. "Do not worry, saying, what shall we eat, or what shall we drink, or what shall we wear … your heavenly father knoweth that you have need of all these things, but seek ye first the kingdom of God and His righteousness, and all these things shall be added unto you."[18] The Lord wants us to ask specific questions because he wants to give specific answers. Over twenty times in the New Testament we are told to ask, seek, and knock. James tells us that we have not because we don't ask. "If any of you lack wisdom, you should ask God, who gives generously to all without finding fault, and it will be given to you but when you ask you must believe and not doubt."[19]

A final key to his direction is to watch for providential workings. Be aware of when a door is opened, and do not be so focused on the door that just shut to not see the one that just opened. Oftentimes God doesn't show us more than we need to know. A great example of this was Peter's experience in prison. James, the brother of John, had recently been put to death with the sword. Herod then seized Peter, who was placed under the guard of sixteen soldiers. Bound in chains and sleeping with soldiers on each side, an angel appeared and told Peter to get up, and when he did, the chains fell off Peter's wrist. Next the angel told him to put on his clothes, and then Peter followed the angel out of the prison cell doors, and he continued to follow his guide to the city gate, and it opened, and they went through it. The Lord opened the door to his cell, the Lord opened the door to the prison, and the Lord opened the city gate.

As much as we would sometimes like to know things in advance, God doesn't show us more than we need to know. God wants us to trust that the right door will be opened at the right time. Our task is to follow and trust that he will open the door. The way God guides us is his responsibility. Our responsibility is to keep informed and listening. We need to keep our minds prepared by the Holy Spirit so that we are not surprised by the touch of God in our lives.

Can we have clarity in our decisions? Yes, we can. Will we always have clarity in our decisions? Not always. I may not always have clarity, but what I have always had is trust in my God. It is when we look back that we have clarity and see that along life's journey he was guiding us. In the unknowns of life, seek his will, listen for that still small voice, focus on his direction, study his Holy Word, ask for the wise advice of others, and after doing all of the above, go with your innermost feelings, your drive, your passion, and the unique gifts God has given you.

As we age, we need God's guidance just as much as ever. The walk of faith is a holy partnership. God promises that he will give you guidance and the inner sense of what you should be doing and where you need to go.

> This God is our God for ever and ever: he will be our guide even unto death.[20]

> Thou shalt guide me with thy counsel, and afterward receive me to glory.[21]

> He leadeth me in the paths of righteousness for his name's sake. Yea, though I walk through the valley of the shadow of death, I will fear no evil: for thou art with me: thy rod and thy staff they comfort me.[22]

Oh yes, that phone call I received this morning about a new direction in life at the age of sixty-five. I followed the advice given in this chapter, I read my Bible, I prayed, I sought the counsel of close friends, I looked for providential signs, and I listened to that still small voice that said a door has been opened for you, and God's will is that you walk through the door and use the gifts God has given you, and make a positive impact on young lives. Is God your guide? He wants to be. Do you have a plan? God does. Can you find the direction he wants you to go? Undoubtedly. For his Word is definitely a lamp for my feet and a light for my path.

NOTES

Two versions of the Bible were used: the King James Version and the New International Version. Unless marked NIV, scriptures are from the King James Version.

Strength Notes

1   Isaiah 6:11–12.
2   Psalm 28:7.
3   1 Samuel 17:26.
4   1 Samuel 17:45–46.
5   1 Samuel 17:47.
6   Psalm 18:1.
7   Psalm 46:1.
8   Psalm 59:17.
9   Psalm 31:2.
10 2 Corinthians 12:9.
11 2 Corinthians 4:7.
12 Isaiah 40:29.
13 Hebrews 12:1.
14 Galatians 6:9.
15 Psalm 73:26.
16 Matthew 17:20.
17 Isaiah 40:4.
18 Jeremiah 16:19.
19 Romans 8:31.
20 Isaiah 40:31.

Love Notes

1   John 13:34–35.
2   Romans 5:8.
3   Galatians 5:22.
4   1 John 4:18.
5   Matthew 22:37–39.
6   Leviticus 19:34.
7   1 John 4:21.
8   Galatians 5:13.
9   Matthew 5:41.
10   Philippians 2:4.
11   1 Peter 2:17.
12   Matthew 25:40.
13   Isaiah 6:8.
14   Philippians 2:3.
15   Matthew 20:28.
16   Ecclesiastes 4:12.
17   John 13:34.
18   John 13:35.
19   Deuteronomy 6:5.
20   Deuteronomy 7:13

Peace Notes

1   Jeremiah 6:14.
2   Isaiah 59:8.
3   2 Peter 1:2.
4   Matthew 11:28–29.
5   John 14:27.
6   Romans 8:28.
7   Matthew 8:25.
8   Matthew 8:26.
9   Psalm 4:8.
10   1 Peter 5:7.
11   Psalm 23:4.
12   Romans 12:17–21.
13   Hebrews 12:14.
14   Romans 12:18.

15 John 16:33.
16 Isaiah 55:12.
17 Romans 15:13.
18 Luke 2:14.

Wisdom Notes

1   1 Kings 3:9
2   1 Kings 3:11–13.
3   Isaiah 55:8–9.
4   Psalm 147:5.
5   Proverbs 2:6.
6   James 3:17.
7   Luke 2:52.
8   Matthew 7:24–27.
9   Luke 14:10–14.
10 James 1:5.
11 Psalm 119:73.
12 Ecclesiastes 2:26.
13 Proverbs 18:15.
14 Proverbs 20:5.
15 Proverbs 13:20.
16 Proverbs 15:12.
17 Job 12:12.
18 Proverbs 16:16.
19 Proverbs 25:12.
20 Proverbs 4:6–7.
21 Proverbs 28:26.
22 Proverbs 23:23.
23 Ecclesiastes 8:1.

Endurance Notes

1   1 Corinthians 10:13 (NIV).
2   Hebrews 12:1.
3   Romans 5:3–4 (NIV).
4   Philippians 4:13.
5   1 Corinthians 9:24 (NIV).
6   Galatians 6:9.
7   Job 1:3 (NIV).
8   Job 1:21 (NIV).

9   Job 12:13.

10 Job 42:12.

11 Psalm 52:1.

12 Psalm 100:5.

13 Psalm 138:8.

14 1 Peter 1:25.

15 Colossians 1:11 (NIV).

16 James 1:2–3 (NIV).

17 Hebrews 10:36 (NIV).

18 James 1:12.

19 Hebrews 12:12.

20 2 Timothy 4:5 (NIV).

Humility Notes

1   Philippians 2:8.

2   1 Peter 5:5–6.

3   Matthew 23:12.

4   James 4:10.

5   Matthew 5:5.

6   James 3:16.

7   Philippians 2:3–4.

8   Proverbs 11:2.

9   Proverbs 18:12.

10 Proverbs 29:23.

11 Proverbs 22:4.

12 Ephesians 4:2.

13 Colossians 3:12.

14 Proverbs 19:20.

15 Psalm 25:9.

16 James 4:6.

17 Matthew 11:29.

18 James 1:21.

Contentment, Peace, Purpose, Confidence, Abundance Notes

1   Philippians 4:11–13.

2   Psalm 51:1–2 (NIV).

3   Isaiah 43:1–3.

4   John 10:10 (NIV).

Giving Notes

1   Romans 8:32 (NIV)
2   James 1:5 (NIV)
3   John 14:27
4   Psalm 37:4.
5   James 1:17.
6   Romans 6:23.
7   Ephesians 2:8 (NIV).
8   2 Corinthians 9:15.
9   1 Corinthians 10:31.
10 2 Corinthians 9:13 (NIV).
11 Matthew 5:42 (NIV).
12 Deuteronomy 16:17.
13 Proverbs 21:26.
14 Luke 3:11.
15 Matthew 2:11.
16 Mark 12:43–44 (NIV).
17 2 Corinthians 9:7 (NIV).
18 Matthew 10:8.
19 Deuteronomy 15:10 (NIV).
20 1 Timothy 6:17–19.
21 Luke 6:38 (NIV).
22 Proverbs 11:25 (NIV).
23 Proverbs 22:9 (NIV).
24 Matthew 6:3–4 (NIV).
25 2 Corinthians 9:7–8.

Gratitude Notes

1   2 Corinthians 9:15
2   Exodus 32:29.
3   Psalm 106:1.
4   Psalm 118:1.
5   Psalm 103:1–2.
6   Genesis 39:9.
7   Genesis 39:22.
8   Ecclesiastes 7:14 (NIV).
9   Genesis 41:16.
10 Genesis 41:39.
11 Genesis 45:5.

12 Genesis 50:20.

13 Colossians 1:15.

14 2 Corinthians 3:18 (NIV).

15 Ephesians 4:24 (NIV).

16 Luke 23:34.

17 Luke 23:43.

18 John 19:30.

19 Luke 23:46.

20 Philippians 2:6–7 (NIV).

21 John 3:16.

22 1 Timothy 6:6.

23 Ephesians 5:20.

Hope Notes

1 Jeremiah 1:5.

2 Deuteronomy 31:8.

3 Psalm 62:5 (NIV).

4 Psalm 71:5.

5 Psalm 131:3 (NIV).

6 Ecclesiastes 9:4.

7 Romans 15:13.

8 Proverbs 23:17.

9 Proverbs 24:14.

10 Ephesians 2:10.

11 Ephesians 6:10.

12 Joshua 3:5.

13 Colossians 4:17.

Faith Notes

1 Genesis 12:1–2.

2 Genesis 12:4.

3 Hebrews 11:19.

4 Daniel 3:17–18.

5 Matthew 9:27–30.

6 Matthew 21:22.

7 Mark 11:24.

8 Luke 1:37.

9 1 Thessalonians 5:24.

10 2 Thessalonians 3:3.

11 Hebrews 10:23.
12 Galatians 6:9 (NIV).
13 Philippians 1:6.
14 James 1:5–6 (NIV).
15 Hebrews 11:6.
16 Matthew 7:7.
17 1 John 5:14.
18 James 2:15–17 (NIV).
19 Romans 10:17.
20 Matthew 26:39.
21 Revelation 2:10.

Guidance Notes

1 John 16:13.
2 Acts 8:30–31.
3 Isaiah 42:16.
4 Isaiah 49:10.
5 Isaiah 58:11.
6 Psalm 31:3.
7 Psalm 5:8.
8 Psalm 25:5.
9 Psalm 61:2.
10 Psalm 143:10.
11 Deuteronomy 31:8.
12 Isaiah 49:11.
13 Proverbs 11:14.
14 Proverbs 11:3.
15 Psalm 16:7 (NIV).
16 Proverbs 3:5–6.
17 Psalm 32:8–9 (emphasis added).
18 Matthew 6:31–33.
19 James 1:5–6 (NIV).
20 Psalm 48:14.
21 Psalm 73:24.
22 Psalm 23:3–4.

Lightning Source UK Ltd.
Milton Keynes UK
UKHW041302171220
375314UK00007BA/340/J